teach yourself

gardening

jane mcmorland hunter
with louise carpenter

For over 60 years, more than 40 million people have learnt over 750 subjects the **teach yourself** way, with impressive results.

be where you want to be
with **teach yourself**

ii

For UK orders: please contact Bookpoint Ltd., 130 Milton Park, Abingdon, Oxon OX14 4SB.
Telephone: (44) 01235 827720. Fax: (44) 01235 400454. Lines are open from 09.00–18.00, Monday to Saturday, with a 24-hour message answering service. You can also order through our website www.madaboutbooks.com

For U.S.A. order enquiries: please contact McGraw-Hill Customer Services, P.O. Box 545, Blacklick, OH 43004-0545, U.S.A.
Telephone: 1-800-722-4726. Fax: 1-614-755-5645.

For Canada order enquiries: please contact McGraw-Hill Ryerson Ltd., 300 Water St, Whitby, Ontario L1N 9B6, Canada.
Telephone: 905 430 5000. Fax: 905 430 5020.

Long renowned as the authoritative source for self-guided learning – with more than 30 million copies sold worldwide – the *Teach Yourself* series includes over 300 titles in the fields of languages, crafts, hobbies, business and education.

British Library Cataloguing in Publication Data
A catalogue record for this title is available from The British Library

Library of Congress Catalog Card Number: On file

First published in UK 2003 by Hodder Headline Ltd., 338 Euston Road, London, NW1 3BH.

First published in US 2003 by Contemporary Books, A Division of The McGraw-Hill Companies, 1 Prudential Plaza, 130 East Randolph Street, Chicago, IL 60601 U.S.A.

The 'Teach Yourself' name is a registered trade mark of Hodder & Stoughton Ltd.

Copyright © 2003 Jane McMorland Hunter

Typeset by Dorchester Typesetting Group Ltd
Printed in Dubai for Hodder & Stoughton Educational, a division of Hodder Headline Ltd., 338 Euston Road, London NW1 3BH by Oriental Press.

Impression number   10 9 8 7 6 5 4 3 2 1

Year   2009 2008 2007 2006 2005 2004 2003

Note: This book largely follows organic principles but does not ignore the use of chemicals. Organic methods are obviously better for the environment and are safer; they can even be easier and in many cases just as efficient as inorganic methods. However, not everyone wants to recycle everything and make their own compost, so throughout the book, where appropriate, both approaches are described.

contents

introduction

Gardening can be one of the most pleasurable and satisfying activities. It has been practised by man since ancient times and can now be traced to almost all regions of the world. At first it may seem intimidating, but in fact an enormous amount of gardening simply relies on common sense and the rest is easily learnt. This book assumes no prior knowledge of gardening and in straightforward steps explains clearly what you need to know to create and maintain a garden that suits you. It is also designed to be used as a handy reference book for more experienced gardeners who want information on a particular subject.

To the beginner, gardening can appear to be a minefield

a typical country garden with a central lawn and surrounding beds with trees, shrubs and flowers

of Latin names and unintelligible terms. In fact you probably already know more than you think. Many people can recognize the flowers indicated by the Latin words *Fuchsia*, *Delphinium* and *Iris*, and it only takes common sense to translate the Latin *Lilium* and *Rosa* into lilies and roses. Libraries may be filled with books on subjects such as pruning, but all this really involves is cutting off dead or unwanted parts of a plant. Obviously there are methods and suitable times for pruning that need to be learnt, but again these are easily mastered. A large number of gardening books are available: many appear terrifyingly technical and others simply seem to consist of beautiful yet unattainable images. Do not be put off by this. Much of the technical information you will never need and with a little time and effort you will be able to produce a beautiful garden of your own.

One of the greatest attractions of gardening is that it can be enjoyed by anyone, regardless of their age, fitness, income or training. You do not need to be a botanical expert or wildly creative, and unless you want to, you do not even need to devote much time to your garden. Many plants take moments to put in the soil and many cost little or nothing, but they will provide months or even years of colour and interest in return. In an increasingly hectic and stressful world, it is very satisfying to get so much in return for so little. Your gardening will be restricted by the space you have available but a surprising amount can be achieved in a couple of window boxes, if that is all you have.

Although a great deal of gardening is common sense, there are rules and tricks that make it easier and more rewarding. Experience can be gained by trial and error but this can be expensive financially and physically, and can end up wasting a lot of your time. It is also very disheartening. If you buy a plant that needs bright sunlight, you cannot expect it to thrive in deep shade; it only takes a little research to ensure plants are situated where they will be happy. A small amount of groundwork beforehand is a lot less painful than slowly watching your plant die. One of the aims of this book is to provide the knowledge based on experience that will save you from making easily avoidable mistakes.

The beginning of the book is aimed at finding out what you want from your garden. It is important to remember that you are more likely to succeed at something if you enjoy it and that gardening should be enjoyable. The next two chapters show you how to assess what you already have in your garden and how to convert it into what you want. Chapter 4 describes the tools you will need and Chapters 5 and 6 introduce you to the basic planting elements of the garden and how they can be used. Chapter 7 describes the techniques involved in creating and looking after your garden. Gardens do not occur naturally but are a result of the interaction between man and nature. It is here that we see how remarkably forgiving nature is. An amazing number of plants will flourish even if not in their ideal habitat and many more will survive months or even years of neglect.

Exact instructions as to when to carry out a particular task are not given as seasons vary and the weather can change from day to day. Spring does not always come when it is expected, and a sudden heavy downpour can waterlog the soil and make planting seedlings out impossible. Also, within reason, there is no right or wrong time to do a particular job. As long as you do things at roughly the right time, it is actually more important to do them when you have the time and inclination to do them properly.

Chapters 8, 9 and 10 cover the more distinct subjects of container gardening, the structural aspects in the design of your garden and the kitchen garden. A season-by-season chart reminds you when you should be doing things.

Finally, useful books, websites and places of interest are listed to inspire you to go even further and a glossary explains terms used. The aim of this book is not only to teach you *how* to garden but also to show you how to *enjoy* gardening. If gardening is seen as an extension of housework or as a weekly chore that has to be ticked off the list, then the real joy of it is lost. With the help of this book you can work out for yourself what kind of garden is right for you and then go on to turn your dream garden into a reality.

latin names explained

Although the Latin names of plants may seem very complicated, there is actually an easy logic to them and the great advantage of using them is that they are part of a universal plant labelling system. This system was devised by Linnaeus (a Swedish botanist who is regarded as the founder of modern botany) in 1753 at a time when Latin was the language of science and was also the only international language.

Plants are grouped together in a Genus, which is usually the first name on a label and is in italics with a capital or capitals throughout, e.g. *Clematis*. Genera are brought together in larger groups still (families), but these are not so important from a horticultural point of view and the family is rarely given in plant lists or on labels.

The individual plants within the genus are called species, and this part of the plant's name is often descriptive, e.g. *Clematis montana* (from mountains). This can be a useful indicator of the sort of conditions the plant would thrive in, such as *maritima* (by the sea), *nivali* (growing near snow) or *himalayensis* (from the Himalayas). If several plants of the same genus are listed together, the genus is represented by its first letter, e.g. *Clematis alpina*, *C. montana*, *C. cirrhosa*, etc.

If the species needs to be broken down further the subspecies (ssp) or the variety (var.) follows the name. These parts of the name are also usually given in italics or capitals, e.g. *Clematis montana* var. *rubens*.

Cultivars are cultivated varieties that differ horticulturally but not botanically – colour or the breeder's name being the most common features of cultivars. The name is not given in Latin (apart from some older cultivars), is printed in normal type and has single quotation marks, e.g. *Clematis macropetala* 'Markham's Pink'.

A hybrid is a plant that is the offspring of two different plants. If it is a mixture of two species of the same genus, this is indicated by an 'x', e.g. *Clematis x durandii*. The two species are not necessarily both listed. If the hybrid genus involves the interbreeding of two genera, the X appears before the name, e.g. *x cupressolyparis*.

Throughout the text plants are referred to by their common names, e.g. snapdragon, and their Latin names are used only when the plant is usually known by its Latin name, e.g. *Phlox*.

All plant lists are listed alphabetically according to the Latin, but any common names are given in brackets.

acknowledgements

Firstly I must thank Hare, John and my parents for encouraging me to garden and allowing me free rein in their various properties.

My agent, Teresa Chris, has been a constant source of support and enthusiasm and my editors at Hodder, Sue Hart and Catherine Coe, have made writing the book a pleasure.

Sue Gibb has given much horticultural advice. Any remaining mistakes are mine, but without her help there would have been many more.

Julie Apps, Barry Delves, Sue Dunster, Mark Hammet, Paul Honor, David Piachaud and Karin Scherer have all encouraged me along the way.

The greatest thanks of all must go to my long-suffering co-author, Louise Carpenter, without whom the book would not have been nearly so much fun to do.

what sort of gardener are you?

In order to enjoy gardening you need first to spend a little time working out what you want to get out of it. Imagine how you would like your garden to look and then balance that against the practicalities of your way of life. The amount of time and money you want to invest in the garden is obviously a key factor, as is the condition, site and aspect of the garden itself. Finally you need to consider how much physical labour you can or want to put into gardening.

You can learn a lot by considering other activities you enjoy – if you particularly like cooking and entertaining you could either choose to make your garden an outside room for cooking and eating in or devote an area or even all of it to growing your own produce. You may wish to spend most of your free time sitting in the garden or you may prefer to be more active. Gardens can easily be designed to suit all these requirements but a little thought is needed before you rush out and buy a mass of plants. You will need to consider when you will primarily use the garden and how regularly you will be able to water it. If you go away every weekend and for long periods in the summer you will either need to arrange for someone to come in and water your plants or choose specimens that are tough enough to survive on their own. Vegetables and annuals have to achieve a lot of growth in a short space of time and therefore need constant care and watering, whereas many perennials, roses and shrubs can survive for long periods without water once they are established.

The type of garden you choose to create will also depend on how long you are going to live there and how quickly you want results. If it is a garden that comes with a rented flat, a few containers may suffice. These have the advantage that you can move them around according to the seasons and, perhaps more importantly, take them with you when you go. If you are prepared to let your garden mature slowly you can grow plants from seed and gradually add to what is already there. In any case it is always advisable to leave as much as possible (within reason!) for at least one season so you can see what you have. It is very easy to dig up perennials inadvertently when they have died back for the winter.

This of course assumes that you have some form of garden already established, even if it appears to be an unruly heap of weeds with a couple of buddlejas fighting their way through. If you have a completely blank canvas, such as with a new house, you will have much more scope as to what you can do, but you will have to plan more carefully and you will not be able to blame anything on the previous owners! Various styles of garden are dealt with in greater detail in the design section, but it is worth considering them briefly here so you know what the main options are. In reality most gardens consist of a mixture of styles that can be adapted as the occupants of the household change.

Many gardens will have to cater for the needs of the whole family and for this each person needs to be taken into consideration. Safety is of paramount importance if you have small children so you need to be aware of the potential dangers of features such as ponds and the growing of poisonous plants. An area of rough lawn can

a simple design of a lawn and surrounding beds, but with the added interest of a central feature

labour-intensive type of garden to maintain. For many years this was the most common system of gardening in rural areas and consisted of a mixture of flowers, fruit, vegetables and herbs. The idea was that your garden would supply most of your food needs and would look attractive into the bargain.

For many people with a busy lifestyle the low-maintenance garden is the most practical option. Once established, many plants need very little attention and even if you have limited time you do not need to be reduced to a slab of concrete for a garden. Closely packed shrubs and ground cover plants will largely look after themselves and the areas in between can be attractively paved and will therefore need nothing more than an occasional sweep.

Wildlife gardens are designed to create as natural an environment as possible to attract wild animals, birds and insects. This is actually harder than it sounds as you are trying to recreate a patch of nature in the raw in a confined area. That said, it can be immensely rewarding as new species come into the garden, either to feed or live.

If you wish to provide your own food from the garden on a large scale, you will need to devote quite a lot of time to your garden, and to dealing with the produce when it ripens. The nineteenth-century gardener, Gertrude Jekyll, sweepingly stated that 'every garden should set aside at least a quarter of an acre for potatoes'! While this is out of the question for most people, nearly everyone can grow some produce even if it is only herbs on a windowsill. While shrubs and flowers can look attractive, there is little to beat the satisfaction of harvesting your own fruit and vegetables and taking them straight into the kitchen to cook, quite apart from how impressed your friends will be!

Finally, you may wish to specialize in some way, perhaps by creating a single colour garden or concentrating on an individual species. At this stage you would probably have no idea of such a thing, but that is one of the charms of gardening – you can do almost whatever you like once you find the type of gardening that you most enjoy. Even if all you wish to do is sit in a deckchair and simply *look* at your low-maintenance garden, there is nothing to stop you doing just that and by doing so you will have achieved what you want from your garden.

make a good play area and at a later stage sandpits and plain areas of grass can be converted into ponds and flowerbeds. There is no point in encouraging your children to hate the garden by imposing too many restrictions on them. It is better to organize at least part of it round their needs and gradually convert it to what you want as they grow up. Many children can become keen gardeners if they are given their own area of ground and a little encouragement. Some may overcome their hatred of eating vegetables if they are involved in the growing process. You also need to take into consideration your own age and mobility and that of the rest of your family or any regular visitors. Too many changes of level can make getting around the garden difficult for people who are elderly or have disabilities, while wide paths and raised beds make access easier for wheelchair users.

The cottage garden is probably a less suitable style if you have small children as the design is such that normally all areas are filled with plants; it is also probably the most

assessing your plot

You may well have a definite idea of the type of garden you want to create, but, however determined you are, there are certain factors you will need to take into account to see whether your dream garden is a realistic proposition. To a certain extent, some of these, such as the condition of your soil, can be overcome, but it is always easier, and in the long run more successful, to work with the naturally existing conditions rather than to try to alter them too drastically.

The first thing you will need to look at is the nature of your garden at the moment. What features do you have? Which way does it face? What is the overall terrain like and how large is it? Secondly you will need to review the climate, both in terms of the general area and also any microclimates that may affect your garden or parts of it. The third important consideration is the soil – many plants are not fussy but others will only grow in certain soils and it is worth finding out whether

even on a steep slope it is possible to create an interesting garden

they will survive in your garden before you buy and plant them. Each of these three factors is considered below.

The garden itself

Before doing anything, look very carefully at your garden and what is already in it. (If it is an area of uncultivated soil this will obviously not take long!) Consider the merits of everything in the garden and, in terms of the plants, how well they are growing. If your garden is bare, look at surrounding gardens as this will give you a good idea of which plants will do well in your area. If your garden is already established, you should leave it as it is for a while. In terms of plants, you should ideally wait a spring and summer before undertaking any major upheavals as many bulbs and perennials are not visible above ground while dormant. Also take into account what surrounds your garden, how overlooked it is and whether there are any features you cannot do much about. These would include things such as streams, large ponds, wooded areas or steep slopes.

Having considered the site, you need to take the aspect into account, i.e. which way your garden faces. This will have a great influence on what will flourish. Work out where north is and consider each side of the garden in turn. In the northern hemisphere a south-facing side will get the sun from mid-morning to mid-afternoon and is the easiest site to cultivate. West-facing sides get the afternoon and evening sun which is also good, but in Britain they can be windy areas as they face in the direction of the prevailing wind. East-facing sides get the morning sun and although this may look adequate, it actually does not do much good horticulturally as early in the day the sun has very little warmth. North-facing sides get little or no sun and only shade-tolerant plants will flourish there. However, these areas very often have the advantage of being sheltered.

You also need to make a note of the positions of the sun and shade throughout the day in winter and summer. Particularly in town gardens the difference between summer and winter may be quite great since in winter the sun may not climb high enough to shine over surrounding buildings.

Climate

The climate of your area will be important, particularly if you want to grow tender plants, but here many potential problems can be fairly easily overcome. If the garden is windy, you can put up windbreaks in the form of trees, hedges, trellis or fences. If you live by the coast you will still have to grow plants that do not mind the salt-laden air, though you can usually grow a much greater range of plants in seaside areas because the climate is more temperate. Consider how much rain you get and what form it takes – does it rain steadily or do you get dry periods interspersed with thunderstorms? In cold areas with heavy frosts many plants can be protected using fleece, straw or newspaper; in some ways frost is a help as it breaks up the soil. Long periods of damp cold are often more harmful to plants, especially those of Mediterranean origin, such as olive trees. Snow is usually protective rather than harmful, but you should always shake it off branches as the weight can be damaging. The temperature range of your garden will obviously influence which plants you can grow and if you live in an area with short summers you are liable to suffer a shorter growing season.

Small areas of the garden may have their own microclimates and these need to be taken into consideration. The bases of walls can be shady and dry if they create a rain shadow, low areas may be frost hollows and buildings or walls can create wind tunnels. You may not be able to do anything about these factors but it is good to be aware of them so you can choose suitable plants.

Soil

The final detail to assess is the soil itself. Apart from peat, all soil is made up of the bedrock beneath it, humus (organic matter), water and air, and of these it is the bedrock that will largely determine its overall characteristics. All soil has a pH level which is a number between 1 and 14 that indicates how acid or alkaline your soil is. Pure water is 7, anything above this is alkaline and anything below is acid. Many plants do not mind what soil they grow in and many people never test their pH levels, but as can be seen from the lists on pages 5–7 certain plants do better in certain conditions. If you want to grow these plants successfully, it is worth testing your soil (kits are available at garden centres and are easy to use). To a certain extent you can tell what your soil will be by its consistency. If it is largely made up of peat, sand or clay it will probably be acidic, whereas chalk and limestone are alkaline. This is useful in as far as it goes, but most gardens are a mixture of soils (particularly if top soil has been brought in from elsewhere) and you may find the pH levels vary quite considerably in different areas of your garden. Neutral soil is anything from 5.5–7.5, but in many ways a slightly acidic soil (5.5–6.5) is best as the acid-loving plants tend to be fussier. It is possible to modify the pH level, but it is not worth trying to alter your soil too much. If you particularly want to grow plants that are not compatible, it is best to grow them in containers with specialist soil. You can make your soil more alkaline by adding lime (calcium carbonate) or calcified seaweed. This should be done in the autumn and you should not plant anything for one month afterwards. Do not add manure at the same time as the two will react and produce ammonia, which causes nitrogen to be lost from the soil. Mushroom compost will also make your soil slightly more alkaline. It is much harder to increase the acidity. Sulphur, leaf mould, pine bark and manure will all make the soil slightly more acidic but the effects will not last long.

You also need to know what type of soil you have as this will determine the extent to which it retains water and nutrients. It is usually quite easy to assess the main soil component by seeing how quickly it drains and looking closely at the soil and feeling it. There are six main types of soil, but remember that most garden soils will be made up of a mixture of different kinds.

Chalk

This is easily recognizable as it usually has small particles of white chalk in it. It drains very rapidly and is alkaline. Normally chalky soil forms a fairly shallow layer on top of the bedrock.

Clay

This is also easy to recognize as it feels slightly sticky when wet and can be rolled into a ball. It has a tendency to get waterlogged, but can also dry out and crack during dry periods. It can feel cold and heavy and be hard to dig when wet, but it holds nutrients well and the texture can be improved by adding organic matter. It is usually acid.

Limestone

This soil is normally full of rocks, which increase as you dig down where the bedrock breaks up easily. It drains very rapidly and is alkaline but not usually to such an extreme extent as chalk.

Peat

This is a dark soil that can hold a huge amount of water by absorbing it like a sponge. It is acid.

Sand

These soils are light in colour and crumbly. They do not hold water well so many nutrients are washed away and need to be regularly replaced. It is usually acid.

Loam

This would be every gardener's dream soil. It is a mixture of sand and clay with a good percentage of humus and a neutral pH.

As stated earlier, many plants are remarkably unfussy, but certain types do better in particular conditions and these are listed below.

Acid soils (clay, peat and sand)
Trees
Betula (Birch)
Fagus sylvatica (Common beech)
Ilex aquifolium (Holly)
Populus (Aspen)
Quercus (Oak)

Shrubs
Azalea
Calluna (Heather)
Camellia
Erica (Heather)
Hydrangea macrophylla (for blue flowers)
Kalmia Latifolia (Mountain laurel/Calico bush)
Pieris
Rhododendron

Perennials
Gentiana
Phlox

Meconopsis betonicifolia (Himalayan poppy)
M. Cambrica (Welsh poppy)
Trillium grandiflorum

Alkaline soils (chalk and limestone)
Most flowering shrubs and perennials will do well.

Trees
Acer – most types (Maple)
Crataegus (Hawthorn)
Laburnum
Malus (Crab apple)
Prunus (Flowering cherry)
Sorbus aria (Whitebeam)
S. aucuparia (Mountain ash or Rowan)

Shrubs
Berberis
Buddleja
Choisya
Cistus (Rock rose)
Clematis
Cotoneaster
Escallonia
Eleagnus
Euonymus
Ilex (Holly)
Jasminium (Jasmine)
Magnolia
Philadephus (Mock orange)
Potentilla
Pyracantha (Firethorn)
Rosmarinus (Rosemary)
Santolina (Lavender cotton)
Senecio
Spirea
Syringia (Lilac)
Viburnum

Perennials
Achillea (Yarrow)
Aquilegia
Aubretia
Bergenia (Elephant's ear)
Campanula glomerata
Convallaria majalis (Lily-of-the-valley)
Dianthus (Pinks)
Fuchsia

Iris
Penstemon
Salvia sylvestris
Scabiosa caucasica
Veronica (Speedwell)

Annuals and bulbs
Calendula officinalis (Pot marigold)
Chionodoxa (Glory-of-the-snow)
Crocus
Cyclamen
Lavatera trimestris (Annual mallow)
Lobularia maritima (Sweet alyssum)
Muscari (Grape hyacinth)
Narcissus (Daffodil)
Tulipa (Tulip)

Clay soils
Trees
Acer (Maple)
Crataegus (Hawthorn)
Laburnum
Prunus (Flowering cherry)
Sorbus (Mountain ash/Whitebeam)
Taxus baccata (Yew)

Shrubs
Berberis
Chaenomeles (Japonica)
Choisya
Cornus (Dogwood)
Cotoneaster
Escallonia
Kerria japonica
Philadelphus (Mock orange)
Potentilla
Pyracantha (Firethorn)
Rhododendron
Rosa (Rose)
Spirea
Syringia (Lilac)
Viburnum
Weigela

Perennials
Aconitum (Monkshood)
Aster (Michaelmas daisy)
Astilbe

Bergenia
Campanula
Digitalis (Foxglove)
Geranium (Cranesbill)
Hosta
Monarda (Bergamot)
Primula
Pulmonaria

Sandy soils
Trees
Betula (Birch)

Shrubs
Berberis
Cistus (Rock rose)
Cotoneaster
Cytisus (Broom)
Escallonia
Hypericum (St John's wort)
Lavatera
Lavendula (Lavender)
Rosmarinus (Rosemary)
Senecio

Perennials
Acanthus spinosus (Bear's breeches)
Centrantus ruber (Red valerian)
Foeniculum vulgare (Fennel)
Origanum vulgare (Oregano)
Papaver orientale (Oriental poppy)
Penstemon

Annuals and bulbs
Antirrhinum (Snapdragon)
Crocus
Impatiens (Busy Lizzie)
Iris
Limnanthes douglasii (Poached egg plant)
Lobularia maritima (Sweet alyssum)
Muscari (Grape hyacinth)
Narcissus (Daffodil)

Windy sites
Trees
Acer (Maple)
Crataegus (Hawthorn)

Laburnum
Sorbus aria (Whitebeam)
S. aucuparia (Mountain ash or Rowan)
Taxus (Yew)

Shrubs
Berberis
Buddleja globosa
Buxus sempervirens (Box)
Choisya
Cornus (Dogwood)
Erica (Heather)
Eleagnus
Escallonia
Euonymus
Ilex aquifolium (Holly)
Philadelphus (Mock orange)
Potentilla
Spirea japonica
Viburnum

Perennials
Centaurea (Cornflower)
Centrantus ruber (Red valerian)
Dianthus (Pinks)
Geranium (Cranesbill)
Lathyrus latifolius (Perennial pea)

Shady sites
Shrubs
Buxus sempervirens (Box)
Eleagnus
Euonymus
Hedera (Ivy)
Hydrangea
Ilex aquifolium (Holly)
Jasminum nudiflorum (Winter jasmine)
Lonicera (Honeysuckle)
Mahonia
Osmanthus burkwoodii
Pieris
Prunus laurocerasus (Cherry laurel)
Rhododendron
Skimmia japonica
Viburnum
Vinca Major and *Minor* (Periwinkle)

Perennials
Ajuga reptans (Bugle)
Alchemilla mollis (Lady's mantle)
Anenome
Aquilegia
Astilbe
Brunnera macrophylla (Forget-me-not)
Convallaria majalis (Lily-of-the-valley)
Dicentra spectabilis (Bleeding heart)
Euphorbia (Spurge)
Geranium macrorrhizum (Cranesbill)

Helleborus
Hosta
Lamium maculatum (Deadnettle)
Primula
Pulmonaria
Saxifragia urbium (London pride)

Annuals and bulbs
Galanthus (Snowdrop)
Impatiens (Busy Lizzie)
Nicotiana (Tobacco plant)

designing your garden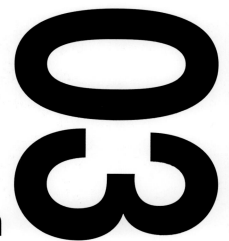

As explained in Chapter 1, there are many different ways of designing a garden and it is important that you choose the one that is right for you, your family and your lifestyle in general.

Even if you move into a house with an established garden, it is worth taking time to consider whether it suits you and your needs. You might find that you want to make changes, maybe a few, maybe a lot, but these do not need to be all done at once. Changes involving plants are usually best made in spring or autumn, whereas structural features, such as patios and paths, can be done at any time. If your garden is bare or needs serious renovation then the planning stage is vital. Ideally you should make a scale drawing of the plot, taking into account such factors as soil, aspect, etc. This is all covered in Chapter 2. If you like drawing, you will find this stage enjoyable. If you don't, simply get a sheet of paper, roughly draw the shape of the garden and mark where you want your principle features to go. At this stage it is enough just to write 'lawn', 'bed', 'kitchen garden', 'patio', etc. When you mark it out on the actual site you will get a better idea of how it will look. If you have a very precise style in mind, such as a formal garden, then your planning will obviously need to be much more detailed. Once you have decided what you want, mark it out using pegs and string, sand trickled through a funnel or the garden hose. Also take into account the height of any feature and, if relevant, how large it will grow.

For many people it is unlikely that the whole plan will be executed immediately and there is no harm in creating your garden design bit by bit, as long as you are following an overall scheme that will eventually bring the whole garden together. In fact putting your plans into practice in stages is often a good thing as it allows you to make alterations – what you have mapped out on paper does not always turn into the reality you expect. Whatever changes you make it is important that the garden has a unified structure and is not simply a collection of disjointed elements. Try to design it so that the different areas lead into one another – paths, arches, curved beds and even steps are all good links.

It is possible to alter the feel of your garden without major structural changes. Using colour is a good way to achieve this. Hot colours, such as reds and oranges, will make flowers stand out and the garden seem lively, whereas strong blues will make the garden feel cooler, and soft shades, for example mauves, pale blues and pinks, will make it appear soothing and restful.

The following pages will give you an idea of the main garden styles and how to create them. Remember that if you try to copy an exact 'look', you will be restricting the range of features you could include. For example, if you choose to have a formal garden you will have difficulty incorporating a lot of wildflowers or a children's play area. In reality most people have a mixture of styles in their garden, however small it is, but they all usually link up to form a unified picture. The most important thing is to have what you want. What William Morris said of houses could equally be applied to your garden: 'Have nothing in your house that you do not know to be useful or believe to be beautiful.'

Features you may need to take into account in your design include:

- tool/bicycle/car storage
- patio
- barbecue/area for eating
- washing line
- area for rubbish (both household and garden)
- compost
- bonfire
- play area
- summer house/conservatory
- water feature
- swimming pool
- paths
- area for pets
- trellis/pergola
- privacy/noise
- containers
- trees
- kitchen garden
- area for cut flowers
- herb garden
- greenhouse

Cottage gardens

More than any other type of garden, present-day cottage gardens look back with nostalgia to a bygone era when cottage gardeners were largely self-sufficient and lived surrounded by flowers in a pollution-free environment. This may have been the case, but such an image often overlooks the fact that cottage gardens were incredibly hard work. They also evolved gradually over time and so are difficult to create in an instant make-over way.

The theory behind the style was that the garden should provide the cottager with fruit, vegetables and flowers all grown in a limited space, which could also allow room for chickens and maybe even a goat or two! For this reason the plants were placed very close together with comparatively few shrubs since they were considered to take up valuable space and yield nothing in return. Fruit and vegetables were either grown in amongst the flowers or in a kitchen garden area at the rear of the cottage. Every inch of space had to be used and annuals, biennials and herbs were planted to fill in any gaps that appeared.

Cottage gardens look particularly attractive in front gardens where a path leads up to the front door surrounded on both sides by a riot of colour. The paths can be straight but their edges must be softened by allowing the flowers to spill over from the adjoining beds. In keeping with the style, fences should be wooden, but to a certain extent you can disguise unsuitable structures by growing traditional climbers up them, such as jasmine and honeysuckle. All hard materials should be

a cottage garden is one of the most labour-intensive styles
to keep it looking this good would require constant maintenance

local, i.e. cobbles in seaside areas and flint, brick or stone in their appropriate geological areas. Old flagstones can look very attractive if irregularly placed with low-growing herbs or flowers in between them.

An easier compromise, particularly in the back garden, is to have a patio and lawn area surrounded by cottage-style beds. You can also bulk up the back of the beds with shrubs, which will lessen your work considerably. By picking evergreen shrubs you can also ensure that you have interesting-looking beds all year round. Cottage gardens were primarily functional and therefore have a tendency to die back and look somewhat bare in winter when little is being harvested. By using shrubs and bulbs you can extend the season without spoiling the cottagey feel. Winter-flowering jasmine (*Jasminium nudiflorum*) and *Clematis cirrhosa* are useful climbers, and forsythia, hebes and hydrangeas will also provide winter interest with little effort. It is also possible to cheat in other ways, for example old roses are the traditional choice for cottage gardens but most only flower once. Many modern roses will repeat flower over a longer period and are often more disease resistant as well. As long as you choose the types and colours carefully and mix the roses with other flowers they will look perfectly authentic.

Below is a list of plants that will help create a cottage garden. The list is in no way comprehensive and a traditional cottage gardener would only grow plants that naturally suited the soil and site of his garden – there was no question of adapting the conditions to suit particular plants other than to provide the best general conditions possible.

It is best to put the trees, shrubs and roses in first and then plant the flowers around them using smaller plants to fill in any gaps that are left. You can grow your fruit and vegetables in amongst the flowers but bear in mind that when you harvest anything you will create a gap that will need to be filled with something else.

Plants for a cottage garden

Trees
(Small trees are usually best.)
Lauris noblis (Bay)
Malus x robusta (Crab apple)
Prunus (Flowering cherry)
Sorbus aucuparia (Mountain ash or Rowan)
Any fruit trees

Climbers
Clematis, e.g. *alpina*, Jackmanii, 'Nelly Moser'
Hedera (Ivy)
Jasminium nudiflorum (Winter jasmine)
J. officinale (Summer jasmine)
Lathyrus odoratus (Sweet pea)
Lonicera (Honeysuckle)

Shrubs
Buddleja davidii
Daphne
Forsythia
Hebe
Hydrangea macrophylla
Lavatera (Mallow)
Philadelphus (Mock orange)
Ribes sanguineum (Flowering currant)
Syringia vulgaris (Lilac)

Roses
Either old or shrub and climbers, for example:
'Constance Spry'
'Cornelia'
'Felicia'
'Félicite Perpétue'
'Gloire de Dijon'
'Mme Alfred Carriere'
'Mme Isaac Perriere'
'New Dawn'
'Penelope'
'Zéphirine Drouhin'

Perennials
Alcea (Hollyhock)
Aconitum (Monkshood)
Alchemilla mollis (Lady's mantle)
Anenome
Aquilegia vulgaris (Granny's bonnet)
Dianthus (Pinks)
Dicentra spectabilis (Bleeding heart)
Geranium (Cranesbill)
Lupinus (Lupin)
Paeonia (Peony)
Papaver orientale (Poppy)
Phlox

Annuals and biennials
Antirrhinum (Snapdragon)
Campanula medium (Canterbury Bell)

Centaurea (Cornflower)
Cosmos
Dianthus barbatus (Sweet william)
Digitalis (Foxglove)
Erysimum cheiri (Wallflower)
Lunaria (Honesty)
Matthiola (Stock)
Myosotis (Forget-me-not)
Nigella (Love-in-a-mist)
Viola (Pansy)

Bulbs

Crocus
Dahlia
Galanthus (Snowdrop)
Helleborus
Iris
Lilium candidum
Narcissus (try the small-cupped flowers such as 'Merlin' or the yellow and white pheasant's eye – flowers such as *N. poeticus* 'Actaea')

For your kitchen garden, plant any fruit and vegetables and all herbs, particularly catmint (*Nepeta*), chives, lavender, parsley, rosemary, sage and thyme.

Formal gardens

A formal garden is a very different proposition in design terms to a cottage garden. It uses a much smaller range of plants and each one is positioned very precisely in accordance with a rigid overall plan. Formal gardens have existed throughout history. There is evidence that they existed in Ancient Egypt and Persia, although they reached their peak of popularity in Renaissance Italy and seventeenth-century France. The gardens were traditionally large, belonging to royalty or aristocracy, and were intended to represent the triumph of man over nature. Despite this, it is an extremely adaptable style of gardening, suiting large or small plots. Symmetrically designed classical houses suit a formal garden, but so, too, do old rambling houses and even many modern buildings.

The layout of a formal garden should be exactly symmetrical, but this is not always possible because of the direction the plot faces, its level and general shape. It is much easier to create the feel of a formal garden by following the basic rules and adapting them where necessary to fit your particular site.

The design should be based on squares, rectangles, circles or ellipses, and all changes in direction or height should be crisp and clear. Some examples of this are given below:

- Patterns can be created using knot gardens, which are flowerbeds laid out in intricate designs to resemble knots. The edges of the flowerbeds are usually planted with low 20–30 cm (8–12 in) box hedges with flowers in the centre. They were common in England in the sixteenth and seventeenth centuries and examples can be seen at Hampton Court and Hatfield House. Parterres can also be used to create interest. They were popular particularly in France and England in the seventeenth and eighteenth centuries and consisted of a flat terrace, usually near the house, laid out with flowerbeds in decorative patterns. The idea was that they could be viewed from the upper windows.

- Interesting shapes can be created using topiary; either cutting the plants into shapes or training them round a wood or wire framework.

Hedging, lawns and hard surfaces, like gravel, are the most important elements, with flowers taking a secondary role (see the plant list on p. 13.) Water is also an important feature but it should always be rigidly contained within stone or brick edging. Raised pools, canals and simple fountains are all suitable but should be classical rather than naturalistic in style.

a simple, formal design, consisting of well-cut grass, neatly trimmed box and a statue, can look very effective

Everything in the garden should be neat and of good quality – the hedges and any bushes or topiary must be well cut and the lawn should be carefully maintained. Brick walls and black or white trellis provide good boundaries and stone or terracotta planters or ornaments can be used to provide interest and colour. The planters need not necessarily be large, but they should have a unifying theme and be positioned to emphasize the overall design rather than stand out from it. They can be planted with annuals, such as pelargoniums, to give colour to the garden or with ornamental shrubs. Furniture can be metal or wooden but should appear formal rather than rustic or relaxing – it need not be uncomfortable, but a plastic sun lounger will do nothing for your overall design!

Formal gardens actually adapt well to being 'lived in' rather than simply looked at. Patio areas complement areas of formal planting, fruit and vegetables can be grown (at Villandry in France the formal garden is totally made up of edible plants) and even barbecues and swimming pools can be incorporated if you have the space and the inclination.

The easiest way to create this type of garden is to draw a scale plan of your site and mark out the design you want. You can then fill in the patterns using suitable plants according to their soil and light requirements. Once the garden is planted and well established you will simply have to cut the grass and trim the hedges a couple of times a year. At a later stage, if you wish, you can always make the plan more elaborate by creating topiary sculptures, a knot garden or even a maze.

The advantages of a formal garden are that it looks good all year round and is relatively easy to maintain. Moreover it actually lends itself to a variety of styles within the overall scheme since the use of hedges allows you to divide your garden into separate boxes or rooms that can suit any purpose you want. For example, a children's play area, which might jar with the orderliness of a formal garden, could be hidden behind a tall hedge. Equally, if you want some cottage-style flowers, they can be planted in a bed surrounded by a low, neat box hedge. In this way you will maintain the crisp lines of the garden. If you inherit a largely established garden that conforms to no particular style, you can always give it a more formal feel by adding one or two carefully chosen features to it. Two urns marking the top of a flight of steps, clipped lavender hedging round a patio or uniform bushes marking corners can all give a garden an air of formality. By gradually altering and shaping the plants in your garden you can considerably alter its feel without having to do any major structural work.

Below is a list of plants that are particularly useful for creating a formal garden. As with all the lists it is simply a selection and is by no means comprehensive.

Plants for a formal garden

Buxus sempervirens (Box): This is very slow-growing and is suitable for cutting into intricate shapes.
Carpinus betulus (Hornbeam): This makes a good dense hedge and although it is deciduous the leaves have good autumn colour and usually stay on the plant throughout winter.
Fagus sylvatica (Beech): Again, this creates deciduous hedging with good autumn colour.
Hedera (Ivy): Useful for training over shapes. Avoid using variegated types for intricate shapes as the leaf colour will make the whole effect look too busy.
Ilex aquifolium (Holly): Good for hedges and simple shapes.
Laurus noblis (Bay): Best cut into simple shapes e.g. pyramid because the leaves are large.
Lavendula augustifolia (Lavender): Trim regularly. Useful for edging.
Ligustrum ovalifolium (Oval-leaved privet): Grows fast and will need to be trimmed at least twice during summer.
Taxus baccata (Yew): Slow-growing but very dense. Good as a divider or backdrop. Poisonous.
Thuja plicata (Western red cedar): A dense-growing coniferous tree.

Family gardens

This is probably the most common type of garden. It is also the least fixed in style since it needs to adapt all the time to the changing needs of the family members. It is therefore important to design a family garden so that the individual features or areas can be changed without disrupting the overall pattern. For example, a sandpit can easily be converted into a pond once it has outgrown its use, so it is worth bearing this in mind when positioning it initially.

With young children safety is the major priority. Ponds or

water features should be fenced off and the planting of poisonous plants must be avoided. A list of the most common poisonous plants follows, but remember you will also have to be careful using slug pellets, sprays and plant foods.

The play area for young children needs to be near the house or seating area so that you can keep an eye on them, but play areas for older children are better hidden away further down the garden, for your benefit and theirs. Swings, climbing frames and rough grass for ball games can be positioned behind a hedge, if you have room. If you don't you can always make a feature of your children's equipment. You could build the swing into a permanent arch and grow climbers up it when your children no longer want to use it. You could also give them a shed of their own to play in, which would extend the range of their garden activities. Many very attractive ready-made sheds are available now, but be careful not to get one that is too small – a miniature cottage may look sweet but your children will soon be too big to fit in it and when they eventually grow up it will not be much use to you either.

When designing a family garden you need to list all your requirements and then see which ones are compatible. You may particularly want fine display flowerbeds, but you can always plant tough low-maintenance shrubs and then gradually change over to more delicate flowers once the football is no longer a threat. Equally, rough grass can usually be converted into a lawn as long as the surface is fairly flat. Always make the patio larger rather than smaller. It can act as a play area when the grass is wet and if you are eating outdoors you can never have too much space. Position ornaments and containers very carefully. Plants will usually recover from children's activities, but stone and terracotta is more vulnerable. Be sure to provide enough seating and, equally importantly, storage space. Bicycles, toys, paddling pools and soft chairs will all need to be stored somewhere, ideally separately from the tool shed.

Children will view the garden as a play area, but you may find that they enjoy helping you with simple garden tasks like raking up leaves and digging. If you give children their own patch to cultivate and look after, make sure you choose a sunny spot with well-nourished soil. If their plants do not grow well they will soon lose heart and interest. Fast-growing annuals, such as sunflowers, nasturtiums and love-in-a-mist, are all good starter plants. Children will also enjoy growing plants they can eat, for example radishes and runner beans. As your children grow up, you can adapt the garden to your wishes, increasing the number of flowerbeds, adding water features and growing more delicate plants.

Poisonous plants

Aconitum (Monkshood)
Atropa (Deadly nightshade)
Convallaria majalas (Lily-of-the-valley)
Digitalis (Foxglove)
Laburnum
Ruta (Rue)
Solanum dulcamara (Bittersweet)
Taxus (Yew)

Possible features for a family garden

- Patio and barbecue

- Sandpit

- Swing, slide, climbing frame

- Treehouse

- Trampoline

- Wendy house or garden shed

- Rough area for ball games

- Children's planting area

- Pool (paddling or swimming)

- Vegetable garden

- Storage space for furniture, toys, bicycles, barbecue

- Area for pets and cage run

- Hammock

Low-maintenance gardens

By designing your garden carefully and choosing the correct plants, you can easily create an attractive garden with varied features for virtually no effort once it has established itself. You will have to plan carefully, and for the first couple of years a certain amount of work will be necessary in terms of planting, watering and training, but after that you should have to do very little to maintain it.

The most important thing is to choose plants that can look after themselves and then to plant them as close together as possible to prevent any weeds growing up in between them. Depending on the size of your garden it may be worth getting rid of the lawn, if you have one. Large expanses of rough grass are comparatively quick and easy to cut, but small lawns with intricate edges are rarely worth the trouble. Paving or gravel requires no work and you can create the effect of greenery by planting low-maintenance evergreen shrubs or grasses. If you do have a lawn, let the grass grow slightly longer and plant some wild flowers in it to give the impression of a meadow. It will only need cutting once at the end of the summer, but bear in mind that this in itself is hard work. If you want shorter grass and have a choice over the type of grass you grow, go for a mixture that is predominantly perennial rye grass. This is tough and will only need to be cut every seven to ten days. Avoid sharp corners round the edge of the lawn, do not have island beds and try not to have trees growing in the lawn as these are all time-consuming to mow round.

If you want a small area of lawn and do not need to walk across it too much, you could grow thyme or camomile instead of grass. Both look (and smell) lovely and are particularly suited to growing within and around paving stones. They will also only need infrequent clipping to keep them looking good. For a children's play area, you could use play bark as a surface. This is soft, attractive and more hard-wearing than grass.

There are a great many ways of creating a low-maintenance garden and not all need to consist simply of paving stones and evergreen shrubs. If you have a large garden you can divide it into a series of rooms, using hedges or trellis and climbers, and then only garden intensively in one or two of these sections. Natural ponds with plants can require considerable maintenance but a simple pool or even a fountain needs very little upkeep. Fruits should be left to grow as bushes, rather than trained as cordons or espaliers, and any bare soil – wherever it is – should be mulched to prevent weeds growing. Avoid bedding plants since they need replanting twice a year and demand a great deal of watering and feeding in between. Seeds, like poppies (*Papaver rhoeas* and *P. somniferum*), cornflowers (*Centaurea*), achillea, hesperis, nasturtium (*Tropaoleum*) and love-in-a-mist (*Nigella*), which grow quickly and easily, can be scattered randomly round the garden. Bulbs, once planted, should come up year after year. Perennials, like peonies (*Paeony*), will look after themselves and if you choose plants that are suited to your particular environment, they will need a lot less attention than if you try to grow plants that would not normally thrive in your area. Consult the plant lists in Chapter 2 and choose your plants accordingly.

Conifers can provide great variety in terms of texture and colour and look good all year round. Most dwarf varieties are very tough, although they do prefer a sunny site. Grasses can also look interesting, especially planted in gravel or around paved areas. For most grasses all you have to do is cut the stems in spring to make way for the new growth.

Your garden will always need water, but here too there are labour-saving devices. Take time at the beginning to install a really good irrigation system, if possible one that waters the plants with droplets rather than a spray as less water is lost through evaporation in this way. A couple of days spent planning and installing the system at the beginning will save an immense amount of time later on. If you do not want an irrigation system, invest in a hose and outdoor tap and buy an attachment for the hose so that you can feed the plants at the same time as watering them. For plants situated around a paved area, consider creating raised beds rather than having containers. These are easier to plant, hold more soil and do not dry out so fast. They should be on a soil bed to ensure good drainage.

When planning your garden consider how to give it some style as well as keeping it easy to look after. It is particularly important to plan the vertical elements carefully since they make a strong impact on the image of your garden and vary enormously in the amount of care they need. Walls virtually look after themselves, but are expensive to build, fences are much cheaper but need to be treated with a preservative every three years or so. Oak and cedar are the longest lasting wood for fences. Trellis must also be preserved and treated regularly, but bamboo screens need no treatment and last well. Pierced concrete blocks are cheap and require no maintenance and their outlines can easily be softened with climbers.

Hedges can be an easy option if you adopt an informal style and choose plants that do not need too much trimming – escallonia, tamarisk (*Tamarix tetranda*), eleagnus and berberis are all good choices when considering this. If you want a more formal-looking hedge choose beech (*Fagus sylvatica*), holly (*Ilex aquifolium*) or hornbeam (*Carpinus betulus*), which will only need pruning once a year. Avoid box, privet or yew as they need pruning every few months.

The flat surfaces also need careful consideration as they are hard to alter once in place. Paving slabs with well-mortared joints are probably the easiest options, but bricks or concrete are also easy to look after. Decking needs to be well preserved and will need regular treatment. Gravel can be used instead of paving for paths and even larger expanses. If you put down a geotextile sheet, e.g. bonded fibre fleece or woven polypropylene beneath the gravel, weeds will not grow through. For ease of walking the depth should not be more than 2.5 cm (1 in) and the pebble size 6–12 mm (¼–½ in).

Easy plants to grow for a low-maintenance garden

Shrubs

Berberis
Camellia williamsii
Ceanothus thyrsiflorus
Ceratostigma
Cotoneaster horizontalis
Eleagnus – all types
Escallonia
Euonymus fortunei
Fatsia japonica
Hedera helix
Magnolia stellata
Pieris
Potentilla fruticosa
Pyracantha
Rhododendron
Skimma japonica
Viburnum

Perennials

Acanthus mollis
Ajuga reptans
Alchemilla mollis (Lady's mantle)
Bergenia
Digitalis (Foxglove)

Geranium (Cranesbill)
Helleborus
Omphalodes cappodocica
Pulmonaria
Stachys byzantina

Ferns

Athyrium filix – Femina
Dryopteris filix – Mas
Polystichum aculeatum

Grasses

Carex hachijoensis syn *oshimensis*
Festuca glauca
Hakonechlon macra
Miscanthus sinensis
Phyllostachys nigra (Black bamboo)

Bulbs

Chionodoxa (Glory-of-the-snow)
Crocus
Galanthus (Snowdrop)
Muscari (Grape hyacinth)
Narcissus (Daffodil)
For ground cover plants see p. 82.

Wildlife gardens

Leaving a garden to its own devices is not enough in itself to encourage wildlife. A real wildlife garden requires considerably more planning and maintenance than you might expect. Many plants that are ideally suited to attracting wildlife tend to be rampant or self-seed all too freely and can easily take over a large area. Partly because of this it is easier to create a good environment for wildlife in a big garden. This is not to say that you cannot tempt any form of wildlife to visit your city patio, but that the overall plan is easier to execute on a larger scale. It is not necessary to imitate the wild exactly, it is enough to choose the right plants and create some of the right environments. Dense planting is better as it gives the creatures places to hide and live in and, for the same reason, lawn grass should be allowed to grow longer and wild flowers encouraged. It is best to allow the various areas of your garden to overlap each other, i.e. let the grass grow longer at the edges and encourage undergrowth and trees to grow right up to the fringes of any water.

A pond is a vital feature for any wildlife garden. It is not only the right environment for lots of aquatic life, but also somewhere for other creatures to wash and drink. It should be as large and as natural as possible with gently sloping sides and generous planting within it. You could also create an adjoining bog garden. This would link the pond to the rest of the garden.

If you attract the insects that are at the bottom of the food chain, the rest will automatically follow. Putting out food and growing trees and shrubs with edible berries will also attract a range of birds, animals and insects. If you feed birds during the lean winter months they will repay you by eating pests during the summer. A birdbath and table will certainly entice the birds into your garden, but you must remember to put food out regularly and ensure that there is always water in the birdbath. Trellises with vigorous climbers and bushy hedges will provide good nesting sites.

Finally, if you are encouraging wildlife into your garden you must not use any chemical herbicides or insecticides. Feed the garden as naturally as possible – making your own compost heap will help you to do this and will also act as a valuable habitat for many small creatures.

Plants for a wildlife garden

Plants to attract birds

Berberis thunbergii
Cotoneaster
Crataegus monogyna (Common hawthorn)
C. x lavelli
Daphne
Hedera helix (Ivy)
Malus sylvestris (Common crab apple)
M. x Zumi
Papaver somniferum (Opium poppy)
Prunus padus (Bird cherry)
Pyracantha (Firethorn)
Sambucus nigra (Elder)
Sorbus aucuparia (Mountain ash or Rowan)
Viburnum

Plants to attract insects and butterflies

Aster (Michaelmas daisy)
Aubretia
Buddleja davidii
Centaurea (Cornflower)
Dianthus (Pinks)

Escallonia
Hebe (Veronica)
Hyssopus officinalis
Lavendula augustifolia (Lavender)
Lonicera (Honeysuckle)
Menta rotundifolia (Apple mint)
Myosotis (Forget-me-not)
Nicotiana (Tobacco plant)
Oreganum vulgare (Marjoram)
Papaver orientale (Oriental poppy)
Phlox
Sedum
Syringia (Lilac)
Tagetes (Marigold)
Thymus (Thyme)
Viola (Pansy)

A winter garden

It is comparatively easy to grow a beautiful summer garden, but to keep a garden looking lovely through the dark, cold months of winter requires a little more thought and planning. Consider carefully how much you use your garden and how visible it is from the house during the colder seasons. From late spring to early autumn most plants will look at their best and if these are the only times when you look at or use your garden then you do not need to think about the winter. If, on the other hand, your garden is on display all the year round, then the following suggestions might be helpful.

If you have a large garden you can plant one or two areas to provide winter colour and as long as you position them well the eye will be drawn to these areas and away from the rest of the garden which may be largely dormant. In a smaller garden this may not be possible and here it is important, if possible, to choose plants that look good for more than one season. A general backdrop of evergreens is useful and a few variegated plants and one or two splashes of colour will be all that is required to keep the garden looking interesting. Plants with coloured stems, like dogwood (*Cornus alba*), and shrubs that produce colourful berries (cotoneaster, pyracantha, rose hips, holly, crab apples and viburnum) are extremely useful. Variegated plants, like ivy and euonymus, will lighten the garden. Be careful since the leaves can turn plain green if planted in too dark a spot. Many winter-flowering plants are particularly sweet scented, like daphne. Plant these so that you can benefit from both the colour and the scent.

When designing your winter garden there are two important things to bear in mind. The first is that evergreens tend to be more tender than deciduous plants. The latter protect themselves by shedding their leaves in winter, whilst evergreens are at risk, because of their foliage, from too much wind and heavy snowfalls. It is important to shake the branches of any evergreen plants after a snowfall since the weight of the snow can damage the plant. The other point to bear in mind is that most of the pictures you see in books and magazines of winter gardens are taken on days when the garden is looking particularly photogenic. Frosty days with clear blue skies or atmospherically misty days both show winter gardens at their best. In reality your garden will probably be viewed mostly on dull, damp days so do not be disheartened if it rarely matches up to your fantasies!

The plants listed below are divided into two groups although there is a considerable cross-over between them. Most of them are white or yellow-flowered. This is partly because they are the most reliable plants, but also because white looks especially good in the low light levels of a winter's day and yellow is the traditional herald of spring.

a well-designed garden can look stunning on a frosty morning as well as at the height of summer

Plants for a winter garden

Autumn/early winter

Acers: These divide into three groups – American, European and Japanese. The American trees, for example *A. rubrum* (Red maple) and *A. Saccharinum* (Silver maple) tend to grow very large (6 m/20 ft) and are only suitable for big gardens. The same is also true of *A. Pseudoplatanus* (Sycamore), the most common European *Acer*. For most gardens *Acer palmatum* (Japanese maple) is the best choice, giving spectacular autumn colours without growing too large.

Acer disssectum atropurpeum
A. ozakuzuki
A. seriyu
Anemone huphensis
Aster (Michaelmas daisy)
Berberis thunbergii
B. wilsoniae
Carpinus betulus (Hornbeam)
Clematis orientalis
Cotoneaster horizontalis
Cotinus coggygria (Smoke bush)
C. microphyllus
Crataegus (Hawthorn)
Euonymus europaeus
Ilex aquifolia (Holly)
Parthenocissus tricuspidata (Virginia creeper)
Pyracantha (Firethorn)
Rosa rugosa
Sedum spectabile (Ice plant)
Sorbus aucuparia (Mountain ash or Rowan)
Viburnum davidii
Vitis coignetiae (Ornamental vine)

Winter/early spring

Aconitum
Camellia japonica
C. sasanqua
C. williamsii
Chaenomeles speciosa (Flowering quince)
Choiysya
Clematis armandii
Cornus alba (Dogwood)
Crocus
Daphne bholua
D. odora
D. tangutica
Forsythia

Hamamelis (Witch hazel)
Helleborus orientalis (Lenten rose)
Iris historioides
I. reticulata
Jasminium nudiflorum (Winter jasmine)
Mahonia
Narcissus
Pieris japonica
Primula vulgaris (Primrose)
Prunus subhirtella
Viburnum tinus
V. Bodnantense
Viola

Evergreen backdrops

Buxus sempervirens (Box)
Conifers
Euonymus japonicus
Hedera helix (Ivy)
Ilex (Holly)
Skimmia japonica
Taxus (Yew)

International designs

There are, of course, innumerable regional garden designs, many of which can be successfully transplanted thousands of miles across the globe.

Japanese (or Oriental gardens in general) transfer particularly well to almost all climates. Much of the full significance and symbolism in the garden is hard to achieve in the West, but the basic style is easy to recreate and the main elements of simplicity, calm and order can still be achieved. Japanese gardens work particularly well on a fairly small scale and are very suitable for city gardens where low maintenance is required.

Form and texture are more important than individual flowers and the main elements are rock, water and simple planting schemes including acers, bamboos, grasses, hostas and dwarf or slow-growing conifers. However, the garden does not need to be dull as bursts of colour can be achieved using plants such as azaleas and ornamental cherries and almonds. Japanese gardens recreate nature but in a controlled setting. Large rocks, in particular, are positioned to look as natural as possible. They can either have water flowing over or around them or, for the ultimate peaceful setting, gravel raked in patterns.

Islamic gardens have been copied throughout the world for thousands of years. They are particularly suited to courtyards and are usually designed using geometric patterns. Water is an especially important element and the gardens usually have a central fountain surrounded by paving or colourful tiles with plants in containers or raised beds.

Mediterranean gardening is not so much a regional style as a climactic one. The features that dictate the design are hot summers, low rainfall and mild winters. The exact scheme has to be adapted for more temperate climates, but can easily be achieved and works well in areas prone to hosepipe bans as most of the plants are drought resistant. The bright blues, yellows, pinks and oranges used in Mediterranean regions look good against the brilliant sunshine, but can look garish if used in areas with less strong light. Here lavender blues, turquoises and, of course, terracotta should be used. Many of the plants have hairy greyish leaves (e.g. *Stachys byzantina* – lamb's ears – or verbascum) and are surprisingly tough – as long as the soil is well drained they will survive cold winters. Herbs, such as lavender and rosemary, are very important in creating a Mediterranean feel and can either be grown in big terracotta pots or planted in wilder drifts.

Twentieth- and twenty-first century designs

Throughout the twentieth century gardening styles changed and many designers placed an increased emphasis on hard landscaping and moved towards more minimalist planting schemes. This is not to say that plants became less important; they were used in a different way. Rather than beds or borders filled with a multitude of plants, one or two specimen plants were used to create an impact. Notably in America, at the beginning of the twentieth century, gardening was more influenced by landscaping and architectural styles than individual plants. The system worked well in large public gardens but also suited small areas where the garden became an outside room and was architecturally regarded as an extension of the building. The sharp lines of modern houses were complemented by the clean lines of this style of gardening – it was the opposite end of the scale from cottage gardening but was also very different from the formal gardens of the eighteenth and nineteenth centuries.

One aspect that really makes a garden feel modern is the use of hard landscaping, particularly metal and glass. Containers will very easily give a garden a contemporary feel if you use galvanized or stainless steel. Stainless steel can also be used to produce a more interesting reflection than plain mirror, and metal can even be used for the walkways. Glass is now very versatile and is a good medium for sculptures, water features or even for nuggets as paths or infilling. If you have sculptures, ensure that they reflect the overall mood of the garden.

Not all modern gardens are minimalist, but many adopt the policy of 'less is more'. They are often based round a single element – perhaps a sculpture or water feature – with simple and restrained planting. Sometimes only four or five plant varieties are used and are chosen very often for their shape alone. This is why slow-growing plants are so popular with modern-day gardeners. There is a limit to how much you can trim a fast-growing plant – it may then grow even faster. Slow-growing plants hold their shape better. This design style takes a lot of careful thought; if you have less in your garden, then everything has to be very well planned and perfectly positioned. That said, it can be cheap to set up and once in position requires little maintenance.

Other planting patterns that are popular at the moment involve a move away from borders towards a more meadow-like approach. The plants are still often used for their sculptural qualities but are planted much more naturalistically. This style is popular in a number of European countries and mostly uses herbaceous perennials that are chosen to suit the natural conditions of the garden. The advantage of this style is that once established the garden needs little maintenance as it is perfectly suited to its environment.

If you are interested in modern garden designs, good places to go for ideas are the larger flower shows. The Chelsea Flower Show, which is held in London each May, always has at least a dozen big show gardens and many smaller ones. A fair percentage of these gardens have modern themes and although you could probably never recreate the entire garden they are very useful for stimulating ideas.

Sculptural plants
Acer (Maple)
Agave america (Century plant)
Allium christophii
A. giganteum
Buxus sempervirens (Box)
Carex elata
Cotinus coggygria (Smoke bush)
Fatsia japonica
Festuca glauca
Ficus carica (Fig)
Haemamelis mollis (Chinese witch hazel)
Hosta sieboldiana
Lavendula (Lavender)
Miscanthus sinensis
Olea europaea (Olive)
Phyllostachys (Bamboo)
Yucca

Water gardens

However big or small your garden, a water feature will always look good. They come in such a variety of sizes and shapes that you should have no trouble finding one that is right for your garden. All water features need sound construction and many will also need electricity. The construction of such features is beyond the scope of this book and many are better done by professionals, but there is a list of books that will give you more in-depth information on this subject on p. 120.

The most important consideration when planning a water feature is that it fits in with the rest of your garden. A formal pond in the midst of naturalistic planting is liable to look totally out of place. You also need to find out what sort of maintenance your pond would require. Large ponds with plants and fish are often self-regulating, but most others will need regular cleaning – a pond with dirty water and algae will ruin the effect of your garden.

If you want a naturalistic pond it is best to site it at a low point in your garden where water would collect naturally. If you want to create a healthy balance of plants and fish, the pool will need to be at least two metres square (7 ft²). The depth should be 75 cm (2 ft 6 in) and the sides should be gently sloping (20 °). Shallow areas should be included for marginal plants and you could even create a bog garden around it that would allow for a gentle transition from land to water. Bog gardens are usually best sited in a semi-shaded spot and can easily be created by lining the area with polythene

a water feature like this works well on both a large and small scale

that has holes punched in it. Bog gardens do not need to be the extension of a pond, but can look particularly good if situated at the shady end of one. If you have a very wet area, it is frequently easier and a more attractive option to make a feature of it rather than trying to drain it. Natural ponds and bog gardens will encourage wildlife and are a vital element in any garden aiming to do this.

A formal pool should have a sharply defined edge. Laying a surround of paving or brickwork is a good way of creating this. It is particularly important with this type of feature to ensure that the water is always kept clean and the surrounding area well maintained.

You also need to decide whether you want the water to move or not. Still water will add to a feeling of restfulness in the garden, as will gentle movement. Large volumes of water moving fast, like fountains or waterfalls, tend to be exhilarating. Little waterfalls or water trickling over stones work well in naturalistic ponds, whereas fountains or cascades are more suited to formal gardens. If you decide to have a fountain, check which way the prevailing wind blows to ensure that your seating area will not be sprayed on a windy day!

Small gardens are obviously not able to accommodate large fountains, but many water features take up very little space. Wall-mounted spouts, self-contained bowl fountains and water bubbling up through a millstone or pebbles will fit into any size of garden and are easily constructed. Barrels or half barrels filled with aquatic plants are a good naturalistic alternative. If you have a small garden, you do need to consider how your water feature will look in winter.

It is very important to site your water feature correctly. Full sunlight will encourage algae to grow, but deep shade will make it hard for anything to survive. Pools under trees will look unattractive when full of rotting leaves and these may in turn alter the pH of the water and thereby upset the pond plants.

If you have children, safety is of paramount importance. Small children will always be drawn towards water, so any depth at all must be fenced off or made safe. Water bubbling over pebbles or a millstone is the safest option, or a small bowl feature that children cannot reach. If you do have a pond, put a wire grill just below the surface of the water which will not show much and will allow plants to grow through. Ensure the mesh is strong enough to hold a child and is well-embedded at the sides. Natural pools can be made safer by having gentle slopes both above and below the water line. If you have paving around the pool, avoid slippery slabs, like York stone, and ensure it is well secured, especially if it overhangs the water.

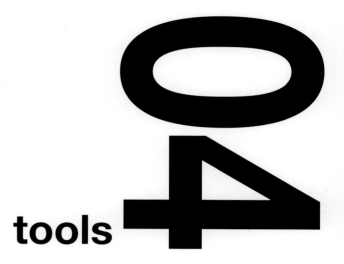

tools 04

Depending on the sort of gardener you are and the kind of garden that you have, you will find some of the tools mentioned in this chapter invaluable and others you will have no use for whatsoever. As a general rule, apart from the basics, like a trowel and a watering can, it is better to wait until you actually need a particular tool before buying it, otherwise you might find yourself superbly kitted out with a range of expensive tools that you never use.

There is a vast array of gardening tools on the market. If you take a look at a Victorian gardening catalogue, you will see that this has always been the case. When buying your tools, choose carefully and bear in mind that on the whole the price will reflect the quality and the length of service you will get out of your tool. Stainless steel tools cost much more than ordinary steel, but they are worth the extra cost as they do not rust and are easy to use. Good tools are essential if you are going to use them a lot. For less frequent use, you would probably do just as well with a less expensive model. Coated steel is much cheaper and lasts reasonably well if kept clean.

Make sure that the tool is the right size for you and that you can use it comfortably. Spades and forks in particular must be the correct height for you.

A final point to bear in mind when buying tools is that while plain wooden handles may look more attractive, brightly coloured ones will stand out more in the garden. It is all too easy to lose sight of a tool you have put down somewhere and it is often a good idea to paint your tools bright colours so that they can be spotted easily.

Trowel

This is the most essential tool for any gardener. As you will use it a lot it is worth buying a good stainless steel model with a comfortable wooden handle. Trowels are available in various shapes and sizes, for example long-handled for those who find bending difficult. They are useful for planting everything except large shrubs and trees, and for digging up all weeds. Narrow-bladed trowels (5 cm/2 in) are particularly useful for small annuals, bulbs and weeds in awkward situations.

Watering can

Whether you have a small balcony or a large country estate, you will find that you need a watering can. Much of your watering can probably be done by a hose, but the jet is often too strong for seedlings and young plants and it is hardly worth hauling the hose through to the front of the house to water two window boxes. Watering cans are available in plastic or metal and for most people the 10-litre (two-gallon) size is manageable. Ideally it should have a choice of roses (spout ends) to give you a fine or heavy spray. Make sure you are easily able to carry it with one hand when it is full of water.

Hose

If your garden is larger than a small patio, it is well worth buying a hose and, if possible, installing an outdoor tap. (You may be able to run the hose from your kitchen sink.) You also need to think about where to store your hose when it is not in use. Hose reels are best for this purpose and can easily be mounted on a wall. A huge variety of nozzles is available, but all you really need is one that will adjust from a single jet to a fine spray. And finally, make sure you buy a hose long enough to reach all parts of your garden.

Sprinklers may seem an efficient and easy way of watering a large area, but in fact most of the water evaporates before it can do any good. Sprinklers also waste a lot of water on areas, such as garden paths, that do not need a good soaking. Far better to buy a folding chair and enjoy the time sitting in your garden with the hose!

Sprayer

Simple sprayers which hold half to one litre (one to two pints) of water are useful either for spraying a gentle mist over small plants or for insecticide, weedkiller, etc. Keep separate sprayers for these different purposes and label each sprayer carefully. Powered or compression sprayers are available for larger gardens.

Spade

Unless you only garden in containers, you will need a spade and even then you may find one useful for transferring compost.

Spades come in various heights and widths and it is vital that you get one that is comfortable to use. The standard height is 71 cm (28 in) but they go up to 90 cm (3 ft). The handles are in the shape of a T, Y or D. The T shape can be tiring to use, but the choice is really up to you.

The blades come in various shapes and sizes and must be sharp to slide easily through the soil. As with all tools, stainless steel ones are the best, particularly for heavy clay soils. Most blades are flat-bottomed but some are curved or pointed. Widths vary from 14 cm (5½ in) to 20 cm (8 in) and the lengths vary also. Larger blades will

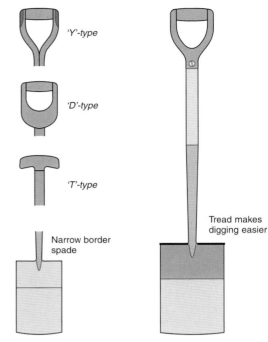

'Y'-type

'D'-type

'T'-type

Narrow border spade

Tread makes digging easier

standard and border spades with tread at the top of the blade
D, Y and T-type handles

obviously shift more soil but will be much heavier to use both as an implement and because of the amount of soil they will displace. Smaller spades are called border spades because they are more manageable for use in a planted border.

Two final points to check when buying a spade is that the socket fixing the blade to the handle is strong and that there is a tread along the top of the blade. This protects the soles of your shoes and gives you a better grip.

Fork

Many people prefer to use a fork as their main digging tool. For anyone with a bad back, they are much easier to manoeuvre in the soil and are useful for more delicate digging – around plant roots, for example. As with spades, forks come in various sizes and may have flat or rounded tines (prongs), both of which work well. Again, match the tool to the amount of work you need to do and to your comfort.

Secateurs

Secateurs must be easy and comfortable to use and they must be as sharp as possible so as not to damage the plant while cutting it. They should be able to cut up to 1 cm (½ in) diameter effortlessly. Check that you can grip the handles easily while wearing gardening gloves, that you can put the safety catch on and off with the same hand and you can still use them easily when they are fully extended. The blades can be either straight or curved. Straight or anvil secateurs may be easier to use, but do not always make such a neat cut. Quality is really important with secateurs, so buy the best ones that you can afford.

Lawnmower

The extent of the grassy areas of your garden will determine what type of lawnmower you need. Anything up to about 75 metres square (250 ft²) can be tackled with a simple cylinder mower that you can push yourself. Any more than this and you will need an electrical or petrol mower. Hover mowers adapt best to uneven ground, whereas a cylinder mower gives a much closer cut. If you want stripes on your lawn, you will need a cylinder mower with a back roller. For this to be a practical option, your grass needs to be fairly short and well-maintained all the time. Cylinder mowers have a series of blades arranged around a cylinder, which cut against a fixed blade at the bottom. Rotary motors have a single blade that turns round, cutting the grass as it turns. They are most suited to dealing with longer grass but can be used for lawns provided you are not aiming at an absolutely flat surface. If in doubt, buy a smaller mower rather than a larger one. Although it will take slightly longer to cut the grass, it will be much easier to manoeuvre.

Strimmers

These are useful for very long grass, for example meadow areas or around hedges and trees where a mower would be awkward to use. They are powered by petrol or electricity and although the electric ones are much lighter, the length of the cable can be restrictive.

Edgers

If you want your lawn to look neat and tidy where it meets paths and flowerbeds, you will need some sort of edging tool. Long-handled shears are useful for cutting grass that overhangs the edge of the lawn and cutters with blades at right angles to the handles will trim the grass near the edges. A half-moon cutter will tidy the lawn and can be used to reshape it. Go easy, though, since each time you use it you are effectively reducing the size of your lawn.

Rakes

A useful general purpose rake is usually about 30 cm (1 foot, i.e. 12 inches) wide with 12 metal teeth, either flattened or circular like large nails. This can be used to collect up stones from the surface of the soil and to break up lumps of soil. If you then turn the rake over, it can serve to level the soil.

A spring-tined or wire rake has a curved head and is mostly used on lawns, either to collect leaves or to scratch out moss. The teeth or tines are much finer than on other rakes and will not damage the grass so much.

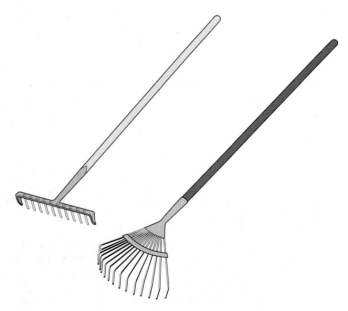

garden and spring-tined rakes

Rubber rakes can be used for collecting leaves in areas that require delicate treatment, such as flowerbeds.

Besom

This is one of the best tools to use for sweeping up leaves and is simply a collection of twigs tied to a larger stick to form a traditional witch's broomstick.

Wheelbarrow

As with many tools, whether or not you need a wheelbarrow will depend on the size of your garden. Most wheelbarrows have a single wheel at the front and two metal legs at the back. Plastic wheelbarrows are lighter to use but not as strong as metal ones. Galvanized metal is probably the most popular material for general use, but you must watch for any rust and treat it as soon as it appears. If you need to push the barrow across the lawn or soft ground a lot, it might be worth buying a ball wheelbarrow or one with an inflatable tyre as this will not sink into the ground so much.

Dutch, draw and short-handled hoe

Hoe

There are many types of hoe, but the best all-rounder is a Dutch hoe. This is ideal for weeding in between plants and even seedlings. By pushing the blade parallel to the soil and just below the surface, the blade will cut off any weeds and avoid disrupting the soil.

The swan-necked or draw hoe has a curved neck and is used with an up and down movement. It will chop out weeds and can be used for breaking up soil and drawing seed drills.

Short-handled hoes are also available and are useful in restricted areas.

Hand fork

These are useful for hand weeding which, in the long run, is more efficient than using a hoe since it removes the roots of the weed rather than just cutting off the top. Flat tines (prongs) are the most efficient to use. Buy the best and strongest you can afford (roots of plants can be maddeningly hard to dig up) and choose the length of handle that you find most comfortable. Short handles give you more control, but long-handled forks will reach to the back of the flowerbed.

Pruning saw

This is used for cutting branches that are too large for secateurs to deal with. It is important to make a clean cut, rather than leave a jagged edge that could attract disease. The most useful is called a Grecian saw and has a curved blade with deeply serrated teeth along the inner side. It cuts as you pull it towards you.

Loppers

These are long-handled secateurs that can be used to cut branches that ordinary secateurs could not manage or reach. In practice, if you have ordinary secateurs and a pruning saw it is unlikely you will need loppers as well. The long handles enable you to reach higher branches, but they can be unwieldly to use.

Shears

These are primarily designed for trimming hedges, but they can be used for cutting small awkward areas of grass round trees, etc. and even for pruning. They should be comfortable to use and not too heavy.

An electric hedge trimmer is only worth getting if you have a lot of hedge. A blade 44 cm (18 in) long will be enough for most hedges. They can be extremely dangerous to use so before you buy one check the safety mechanisms – it should have a hand guard and an automatic cut off if you let go of the trigger. Bear in mind they are tiring to use and very noisy and will not contribute at all to your peaceful afternoon pottering in the garden (or to your neighbour's!).

Bulb planter

This is a useful tool if you want to plant a lot of bulbs as it makes a neater hole than a trowel. However, it will only work in medium to heavy soils as sandy soils do not hold together. They also do not work well in stony soils.

Sieve

These are useful for removing stones from seedbeds and scattering a fine layer of compost over seed.

Equipment for seed growing

For this you will need seed trays or plugs, flowerpots, a dibber for making holes and a widger for moving seedlings (the last two can really be improvised by using a pencil and a lolly stick). You will also need a waterproof marker and labels.

Miscellaneous

This section covers the odds and ends that you will almost certainly need.

Gloves

These are a priority unless you have extremely tough hands. They should come well up your wrist. Although they may seem unwieldly, those with suede patches give much more protection. Full leather gloves are only necessary if you are going to prune a lot of roses.

Knife

All professional gardeners insist you should have a folding knife. If you can use one properly it can be invaluable, but incorrect use of it is also an easy way to damage plants. A pair of scissors or secateurs often work just as well.

Canes

Bamboo and wooden canes in varying sizes will be needed to support some plants. If you do not like the look of bamboo canes you can paint them green or use natural twigs and branches instead.

String

Garden string or ties are essential for fixing your plants to supports. Always make sure that you tie the plants loosely enough to allow them to grow. Soft green string does not last as long as plastic ties, but does less damage to the plants.

Bucket

An ordinary bucket can also be very useful. You can carry compost in it, soak potted plants in it, use it as a mini wheelbarrow when you are weeding and, as long as you keep it clean and dry, you can store your tools in it.

Trug

A more attractive container for carrying your equipment around in is a small wicker basket or a trug. Trugs are flattish wooden baskets traditionally used for collecting fruit, vegetable and flowers. Authentic ones are made from split chestnut and willow and may seem expensive but last a long time and age beautifully. Try to get into the habit of putting your tools back into whatever container you use the minute you finish with them as it is surprisingly easy to lose tools even in a small garden.

Shed

Finally you need to consider where you are going to store your tools when they are not in use. If your garden is small, they will fit in a basket, trug or kitchen drawer, but for anything larger you will need to set aside a permanent storage area. Small upright sheds are very useful and can easily be disguised by climbing plants. Even the smallest will accommodate bags of compost, containers of feed and sprays and allow you to hang your tools up, which is much better for them. Seats with lids are available for storage, but you must not just throw your tools in and leave them in a damp rusting heap.

If you decide to have a shed, get one that is as large as possible as you will soon accumulate a surprising number of gardening accessories. Take care when positioning it to make it a feature of the garden, rather than an eyesore.

Care

Always clean your tools after use. Mud and grass should be wiped off, the metal parts dried and, ideally, non-stainless steel tools wiped with an oily rag. Blades should always be kept sharp and any mechanical tools serviced regularly so that they are both efficient and safe. If possible, hang your tools up – this makes them easy to find and also prevents them becoming damp and rusty.

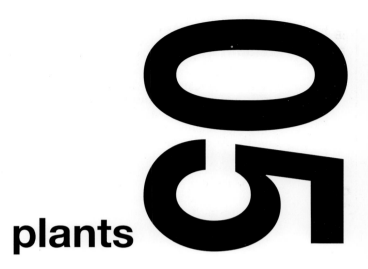

plants 5

Trees

Trees are probably the most dominant and longest-living feature of any garden. It is therefore worth thinking for a time before you either plant a tree or cut down an existing one. A tree will give height, shade and a feeling of maturity to all gardens regardless of their size. As can be seen from the list below, trees come in a great range of sizes and varieties and there will be one that is just right even for a balcony or a roof garden.

Trees may not seem as varied as shrubs but in fact there are things you need to consider before getting one. Do you want an evergreen or deciduous variety, a flowering or non-flowering kind? Some trees have particular features, such as scent, autumn colour, interesting bark or fruits, and this may be what you are looking for. You need to decide whether to plant the tree singly or as part of a group and probably, most important of all, you will need to check its eventual size. When studying plant lists check the sizes given are those at maturity and not just after ten years. Most trees will reach their full size at 20 years, but some will go on increasing in size for a hundred years! The speed of growth varies from tree to tree, but most take about three years to settle in and will not grow much during this time. Remember that the final size will also be influenced by the soil and climate of the area.

Be careful when positioning a new tree. It should not be planted too near buildings (as a rough guide the roots will spread out as far as the final spread of the branches) and you should take into account the shade they will create. Also, depending on the tree, plants may not grow beneath it. In large naturalistic gardens, it is usually best to choose an indigenous species as this will blend with the landscape and encourage wildlife. In smaller gardens your choice may be more restricted by size. If you are using trees as a windbreak, make sure the branches go all the way down to ground level but are not so dense that the wind cannot get through them. What you want to do is slow the wind down, not block its path completely as this may cause it to divert round the tree and increase the problem. Finally, when choosing a tree for a small garden, try to ensure it has at least two seasons of interest, e.g. blossom, autumn colour, fruits or good winter shape. Below is a limited selection of large, medium and small trees that would suit most gardens.

Large trees

	Height	Width
Acer saccharinum (Silver maple)	25 m (80 ft)	15 m (50 ft)
A. pseudoplatanus (Sycamore)	30 m (100 ft)	9 m (30 ft)
Carpinus betulus (Hornbeam)	20 m (65 ft)	3 m (10 ft)
Fagus sylvatica (Common beech)	25 m (80 ft)	25 m (80 ft)
Quercus frainetto (Hungarian oak)	20 m (65 ft)	18 m (60 ft)
Q. canariensis (Algerian oak)	20 m (65 ft)	12 m (39 ft)

Q. robur (English oak) 27 m (88 ft) 25 m (80 ft)

Medium trees

Acer rufinerve (Snake bark maple)	10 m (30 ft)	7 m (32 ft)
Betula pendula (Silver birch)	20 m (65 ft)	5 m (16 ft)
Magnolia x loebneri 'Merril'	12 m (39 ft)	3 m (10 ft)
Magnolia x loebneri 'Leonard Messel'	10 m (32 ft)	6 m (20 ft)
Magnolia grandiflora	15 m (50 ft)	15 m (50 ft)
Malus hupuhensis (Crab apple)	8 m (26 ft)	8 m (26 ft)
M. x zumi 'Golden hornet'	8 m (25 ft)	7 m (23 ft)
M. x robusta 'Red Siberian'	12 m (39 ft)	10 m (32 ft)
Prunus avium 'Plena' (Wild cherry)	12 m (39 ft)	12 m (39 ft)

P. padus (Bird cherry)	9 m (29 ft)	5 m (16 ft)
P. sargentii (Sargent's cherry)	10 m (32 ft)	15 m (50 ft)
Sorbus aria (Whitebeam)	12 m (39 ft)	8 m (26 ft)
S. cashmiriana (Kashmir rowan)	9 m (29 ft)	9 m (29 ft)
S. 'Joseph Rock'	8 m (26 ft)	6 m (20 ft)

Small trees

Acer palmatum (Maple)	5 m (16 ft)	5 m (16 ft)
A. shirasawanum 'Aureum'	6 m (20 ft)	5 m (16 ft)
Crataegus laevitica (Hawthorn)	5 m (16 ft)	5 m (16 ft)
C. x lavelli	7 m (23 ft)	10 m (32 ft)
Magnolia kobus	9 m (29 ft)	5 m (16 ft)
M. stellata	3.5 m (11 ft)	3.5 m (11 ft)

it is important to consider how a tree will look throughout the year

deciduous trees can look attractive even when they have lost their leaves, and trees such as Japanese maples provide a stunning display in autumn

Malus x robusta 'Red Sentinel' (Crab apple)	5.5 m (18 ft)	5.5 m (18 ft)
M. 'Everest'	6 m (20 ft)	4 m (13 ft)
M. toringo ssp *sargentii*	6 m (20 ft)	4 m (13 ft)
Prunus 'Kursar' (Flowering cherry)	5 m (16 ft)	3 m (10 ft)
P. 'Pink Shell'	5 m (16 ft)	4 m (13 ft)
P. 'Kanzan'	6 m (20 ft)	4 m (13 ft)
Sorbus aucuparia (Mountain ash or Rowan)	10 m (32 ft)	3 m (10 ft)
S. forrestii	6 m (20 ft)	6 m (20 ft)
S. sargentiana (Sargent's rowan)	10 m (32 ft)	6 m (20 ft)
S. vilmorinii	4 m (13 ft)	5 m (16 ft)

Shrubs

In the gardening scheme of things, shrubs come in between trees and perennials. They usually have several woody stems and can range in size from low ground cover plants to large bushes. The dividing line between large shrubs and small trees is very vague. Lilac is a typical example that can appear in both lists. Most climbers, roses and soft fruit bushes also fall in the shrub category but these plants are considered separately here.

Shrubs are extremely useful and form the basis for most planting schemes. They can be deciduous or evergreen and many provide good winter interest. They are also useful for hiding unattractive areas such as bins or compost heaps. You can create entire borders of shrubs, mix them with perennials, annuals and bulbs to form a mixed border or plant them singly as specimen plants. Shrubs tend to fall into one of two categories: either providing great interest for a short period of time – e.g. lilac, which looks stunning in flower but only for a few weeks – or forming the main substance of a low-maintenance scheme – e.g. ivy and eleagnus provide year-round greenery and need very little care. The trick is to use other plants to extend the interest – most shrubs can be under-planted with bulbs, and climbers, such as clematis, can be trained through them to extend the flowering period. This way you can easily have colour from early spring right through to the autumn.

Shrubs usually take two to three years to become established, but after that many need little or no maintenance. Pruning is usually the only task and this is covered on pp. 64–7. As with trees, check the final size before planting.

Scented shrubs

Buddleja
Camellia (Small flowering types)
Choisya
Cistus (Rock rose)
Daphne
Hamemelis (Witch hazel)
Lavendula (Lavender)
Magnolia
Osmanthus
Philadephus (Mock orange)
Rosa (Rose)
Rosmarinus officinalis (Rosemary)
Syringia (Lilac)
Viburnum
(For scented climbers see pp. 36–7 and 47.)

Roses

Roses are simply a type of shrub, but they are very important features in many gardens because of their amazing flowers and their range and versatility. At first the choice may seem overwhelming, but roses can easily be divided up into fairly distinctive groups. This makes choosing roses suitable for your garden simpler.

Most roses do best if sheltered from strong winds and grown in neutral or acid clay soil, but many will flourish in poor conditions as long as you enrich the soil when planting.

When choosing a rose you need to decide what you want it to do and which features are most important to you. They range in size from low ground cover plants and patio roses to huge plants that will grow up through a tree or cover a building. Some flower once in mid-summer, others flower in mid-summer and again in autumn and a final group flower almost continuously throughout the summer and early autumn as long as they are regularly deadheaded. Many are strongly scented and others grow interesting hips in autumn. The shape of the flower also varies – single flowers have less than eight petals and are usually fairly flat, doubles tend to be more circular in shape and can have anything from 20–40 petals, and semi-doubles come in between the two.

An important point to bear in mind when planning roses for the garden is that you should not plant a rose on a site where another rose has recently been growing. If you have no choice, you need to remove the soil to a depth of 25 cm (10 in) and replace it. This soil can be used elsewhere in the garden for growing any other plants.

Below are brief descriptions of the main types of roses and a selection of each. This is only a tiny selection and if you become interested in roses it is well worth visiting flower shows or specialist nurseries and talking to the growers as new strains are always being developed. Take time to choose the right rose, in particular check the final height and the background against which your rose will be seen. This is especially important with climbing roses that do not form a dense background for the flowers – pale pink or white flowers will not show up well against a white wall and many pinks and reds do not look good against brick. Colour descriptions are notoriously difficult (one person's salmon can be another's orange) so it is always best to try to see the roses in bloom somewhere if you want a particular shade.

In the listing particular features of the roses are given as follows:

R. = Repeat flowering – depending on the rose and the conditions, the plants may flower in mid-summer and again in autumn or almost continuously throughout the summer up until winter
Sh. = Tolerant of shade
Sc. = Particularly scented
H. = Bears attractive hips after flowering
N. = Can be grown against a north-facing wall

Species

These grow wild in parts of the northern hemisphere and are easily recognizable in catalogues as many usually only have Latin names. They have not been interbred and are the ancestors of most ramblers. Many can be rampant, they only flower once and have small flowers that are strongly scented and later develop attractive hips.

Rosa eglanteria Pink Sc. H.
Rosa moyessii Deep red Sc. H.
Rosa pimpinellifolia 'Grandiflora' White Sc. H.
Rosa xanthina var *spontanea* 'Canary Bird' Yellow Sc.

Shrub and bush roses

Old roses

These are also called heritage or historic roses and were found throughout the Middle East and in Ancient Greece and Rome. They are mostly quite tall (1.5–2 m/5–7 ft) and usually flower once in mid-summer. The scent, colour and shapes of the blooms are the main reasons for growing these roses rather than for a continuous display of colour. They are broken up into groups as follows.

Alba

These are tough plants, which are easy to grow. They come in shades of pink and white and usually have double or semi-double, highly scented flowers that bloom early. They can often be recognized by their greyish leaves. Height and spread 1.8 × 1.2 m (6 × 4 ft).

Rosa alba semi-plena White H. Sc. Sh.
'Celestial' Pink Sc. Sh.
'Cuisse de Nymph' ('Maiden's Blush') Pink Sc. Sh.
'Queen of Denmark' ('Koenigin von Danemarck') Pink Sc. Sh.
'Félicité Parmentier' Pink to cream Sc. Sh.

Bourbon

These are named after the Isle de Bourbon (Reunion) where they were first found in the nineteenth century. They are usually tall, slim plants with white, pink or striped flowers. Their advantage is that they combine the scent of Damask roses with the second flowering of China Roses. Height and spread 1.5 × 1.2 m (5 × 4 ft).

'Boule de Neige' White R. Sc.
'Louise Odier' Pink/lilac R. Sc.
'Madame Isaac Pereire' Deep pink R. Sc.
'Madame Pierre Oger' Silver pink R. Sc.
'Zéphirine Drouhin' Carmine pink Climber 3 m (10 ft) R. Sc. Sh.

Centifolia or cabbage

These are the roses that appear in Dutch flower paintings of the seventeenth century. The flowers are large and highly scented with many petals (centifolia means 100 petals) but they only flower once and the plants are not very robust and may need staking. Colours range from white to crimson. Height and spread 1.5 × 1.4 m (5 × 4 ft).

'Chapeau de Napoleon' ('Crested Moss') Pink Sc. (the buds look like Napoleon's Tricorn)
'Fantin Latour' Blush pink Sc.
'De Meaux' Dwarf pink Sc.
'Robert le Diable' purple/red Sc.

wild dog rose

modern cluster flowered rose 'Iceberg'

english rose 'Graham Thomas'

bourbon shrub rose 'Louise Odier'

China

This group has little scent but flowers from mid-summer until the first frosts. When introduced to Europe in the eighteenth century by the East India Company they were the first roses to repeat flower reliably. The blooms are usually fairly small and can be single or double. Height and spread 75 × 75 cm (2 ft 6 in × 2 ft 6 in).

'Hermosa' Lilac/pink Sc. R.
'Mutabilis' Orange buds/copper/crimson R.
'Old Blush China' ('Monthly Rose') Pink R.

Damask

These are tough plants with highly scented pink or white flowers. They are single flowering apart from *Rosa damascena bifera* 'Quatre Saisons' (Pink), which is the oldest repeat flowering rose. They are elegant plants with arching stems. Height and spread 1.5 × 1.2 m (5 × 4 ft).

'Isphahan' ('Pompom des Princes') Pink Sc.
'Celsiana' Pale pink Sc.
'Madame Hardy' White Sc.

Gallica

These are the oldest garden roses and were first cultivated in France and Holland where they became very popular. The plants are usually short and bushy and are tough and undemanding. The blooms are semi-double or double and fairly flat and range in colour from pink to red to purple. They are highly scented but only flower once. Height and spread 120 × 90 cm (4 × 3 ft).

'Charles de Mills' Deep red with pink and white patches
'Officinalis' ('Apothecary's Rose'/'Red Rose of Lancaster') Pale crimson Sc.
'Rosa Mundi' Pink/crimson stripes Sc.
'Tuscany' ('Old Velvet Rose') Crimson

Hybrid Musk

These highly scented roses were bred in early twentieth-century Britain by Rev Joseph Pemberton. The blooms are white, pink or apricot and produce a second flush in autumn. Height and spread 1.5 × 1.5 m (5 × 5 ft).

'Buff Beauty' Apricot yellow Sc. R.
'Cornelia' Apricot pink Sc. R.
'Felicia' Silvery pink Sc. R.
'Moonlight' Creamy yellow Sc. R.
'Penelope' Creamy pink Sc. R.

Hybrid Perpetual

These roses were popular in nineteenth-century Europe but are not actually perpetual. There is a first flush in mid-summer followed by a second in autumn. They were developed by crossing Portland, Bourbon and China roses and have large fragrant flowers in reds and crimsons. Height and spread 1.5 × 1.2 m (5 × 4 ft).

'Ferdinand Pichard' Pink with red stripes Sc. R.
'Frau Karl Druschki' ('Snow Queen') White R.
'Reine de Violettes' Lilac/purple R.
'Souvenir du Dr Jamain' Maroon Sc. R.

Moss

These roses are distinguished by the green fluff of 'moss', which appears on the sepals and flower stalks. They originated from *centifolia* roses, are highly scented and some have a second flowering in autumn. Height and spread 1.5 × 1.2 m (5 × 4 ft).

'Blanche Moreau' White Sc.
'General Kleber' Mauve/pink Sc.
'Henri Martin' Crimson Sc. H.
'Old Moss Rose' (Common Moss Rose/*x centifolia* 'Muscosa') Pink Sc.
'William Lobb' ('Old Velvet Moss') Crimson Sc.

Polyantha

These are small, hardy bushes that produce clusters of small flowers throughout the summer. The flowers are white, pink or apricot and most have little scent. Height and spread 75 × 60 cm (2 ft 6 in × 2 ft).

'The Fairy' Pale pink R.
'Yvonne Rabier' White R. Sc.

Portland

These are smallish bushes with white, red or crimson flowers, some of which are scented and some of which have a second flush of flowers in late summer or early autumn. They were bred from China, Gallica and Damask roses at the end of the eighteenth century. Height and spread 90 × 90 cm (3 × 3 ft).

'De Recht' ('Rose de Recht') Purple/pink R. Sc.
'Madame Knorr' ('Comte de Chambord') Pink R. Sc.

Rugosa

These were bred from Japanese roses and are easily recognized by their dark green, wrinkled leaves. They are extremely tough and undemanding, surviving happily in poor soils and polluted areas. The flowers are large, white, pink or crimson, mostly fragrant and flower throughout the summer. Some have large hips in the autumn. Height and spread 1.8 × 1.5 m (6 × 5 ft).

'Agnes' Yellow Sc. R.
R. *rugosa* 'Alba' White H. R.
'F. J. Grootendorst' Crimson, frilly petals R.
'Fru Dagmar Hastrup' ('Frau Dagmar Hartopp') Pink R. H. Sc.
'Roseraie de l'Hay' Wine red S. R.

Modern roses
This is a very broad group whose only unifying factor is that all the roses are comparatively recent.

Large-flowered (Hybrid Tea)
Up until 1979 these roses were called Hybrid Teas. The World Federation of Rose Societies changed the name so it was more descriptive, but both classifications are still in use. The plants have a stiff upright growth and were popular in formal rose gardens and for cut flowers. The large conical buds open into floppy flowers that bloom repeatedly throughout the summer. There is a wide range of colours but not all flowers are scented. Height and spread 90 × 75 cm (3 ft × 2 ft 6 in).

'Alexander' Vermilion R. light Sc.
'Elizabeth Harkness' Buff/pink Sc. R.
'Just Joey' Copper/orange R. Sc.
'Peaudouce' ('Elina') Pale yellow R. light Sc.
'Polar Star' Ivory/white Sc. R
'Royal William' Crimson Sc. R.
'Silver Jubilee' Pink/peach Sc. R.

Cluster-flowered (Floribunda)
These were renamed at the same time as Hybrid Teas (see above). They have smaller blooms that appear in clusters throughout the summer. The plants are bushy and fairly tough and provide a very good display of colour although few are strongly scented. Height and spread 75 × 60 cm (2 ft 6 in × 2 ft).

'Escapade' Pinky/violet Sc. R.
'Fragrant Delight' Orangey/pink Sc. R.
'Korresia' Bright yellow Sc. R.
'Iceberg' White Sc. R.
'English Miss' Pale pink Sc. R.
'The Times Rose' Crimson R.

Modern shrub roses
The majority of these are tough plants which mostly flower continuously throughout the summer. They can have single or double flowers and come in a variety of sizes and colours. Some are fragrant, while others have attractive hips in the autumn. Height and spread 60 × 75 cm (2 ft × 2 ft 6 in) to 2.7 × 2.5 m (9 × 8 ft).

'Ballerina' Pale pink, white centre light Sc. R.
'Fred Loads' Vermilion Sc. R.
'Frühlingsgold' Creamy yellow Sc.
'Frühlingsmorgan' Deep pink yellow centre Sc. R.
'Nevada' Cream R. light Sc.
'Cerise Bouquet' Deep pink R.

English roses
Stylistically these roses come in between old and modern and many combine the best of both. They were developed from the 1970s onwards by David Austin in England and new varieties are being added all the time. The best ones have the scent and flower shape of old roses but repeat reliably, are tough and come in a greater range of colours, for example English roses are easily available in yellows and oranges, which are rare amongst old roses. Many are also climbers.

'Abraham Darby' Apricot pink and yellow Sc. R.
'Gertrude Jekyll' Deep pink Sc. R.
'Glamis Castle' White Sc. R.
'Graham Thomas' Deep yellow Sc. R.
'Heritage' Pale pink Sc. R.
'L. D. Braithwaite' Crimson Sc. R.
'Mary Rose' Rose pink slight Sc. R.
'The Pilgrim' Pale yellow Sc. R.

Patio roses
These are a fairly recent development and come in between the miniature and cluster-flowered (floribunda) groups. There is no definite size and according to which book or catalogue you are looking at you may find them classified under either heading. Most are about 45 cm (18 in) high.

'Anna Ford' Deep orange Sc. R.
'Cider Cup' Apricot pink Sc. R.
'Festival' Crimson Sc. R.
'Queen Mother' Pink Sc. R.
'Ray of Sunshine' Yellow Sc. R.
'Sweet Dream' Peachy pink Sc. R.

different types of roses can be planted together to give the garden height and a longer flowering period

Miniature roses

These vary in size from 22–45 cm (9–18 in) and produce equally miniature flowers. As they are so small they do not develop the powerful roots of larger roses and need regular feeding and watering. They are useful for edging, in rock gardens and in miniature beds.

'Little Buckaroo' Scarlet, white centre Sc. R.
'Magic Carrousel' Creamy white Sc. R.
'Mr Bluebird' Lilac Sc. R.
'Yellow Doll' Light yellow Sc. R.
'Stars 'n' Stripes' Red and white stripes Sc. R.

Ground cover roses

These have only been separately listed from shrub roses since 1980 as enough varieties have now been developed for them to have their own category. Increasingly, repeat flowering types are available. Few are scented but this does not really matter as the roses are so low. Check the height and spread and whether the plant is creeping or arching – the height can vary from 20 cm (8 in) to 1 m (39 in). The two main groups are called after counties – e.g. 'Avon', 'Essex' and 'Kent' – and game birds – e.g. 'Grouse', 'Partridge' and 'Pheasant'. Most repeat flower reliably and the game birds group is fragrant.

Climbing roses

Many climbers are similar to large flowering and cluster flowering roses but on very long stems. Most repeat flower and some are scented. They have stiff stems, which form a framework for the flowers but do need regular pruning. Some Bourbons and China roses are also climbers. Choose your rose carefully, taking the site and your requirements into consideration. Most climbers do well against walls whereas ramblers are better suited to draping over small buildings and growing up through trees. Be careful as only some roses will do well against shady walls.

'Danse de Feu' Scarlet N. R.
'Golden Showers' Yellow N. R. Sc.
'Handel' Pink and cream R.
'Iceberg Climbing' White N. R.
'New Dawn' Pale pink R. N. Sc.
'Parade' Deep pink R. Sc.
'Summer Wine' Coral R.
'Zéphirine Drouhin' Carmine pink N. R. Sc.

Rambler roses

These have much more flexible stems than climbers and bear a huge number of flowers in clusters in mid-summer. The display usually only lasts for a few weeks but can be spectacular. Ramblers do best where they can drape over something such as a tree or building and although the flowers do not repeat they are usually very fragrant. These roses only need pruning to control their size, not to increase their flowering, so be careful to choose the correct size. Some, such as 'Wedding Day', are huge and can easily reach 9 m (30 ft).

'Albéric Barbier' Orange/cream N. Sc.
'Albertine' Pink Sc.
'Crimson Shower' Crimson Sc.
'Emily Gray' Pale yellow Sc. N.
'Paul's Himalayan Musk' Lilac pink Sc. N.
'Sanders' White Rambler' White Sc.
'Veilchenblau' Violet N. Sc.

Noisette

These climbing roses were bred in America at the beginning of the nineteenth century by Philippe Noisette and are a cross between a China and a Musk rose. They are fragrant and repeat flowering with silky petals in shades of white and cream. They are not common now as not all are fully hardy and most need a warm sheltered wall. The exception is 'Madame Alfred Carriere' which has pinkish white flowers, is highly scented, repeat flowers and will grow against a shady wall. Height and spread 6 m (20 ft).

'Blush Noisette' Lilac/pink Sc. R.
'Gloire de Dijon' Buffy yellow/pink Sc. R.

Perennials

The strict definition of a perennial is a plant that lives for more than three seasons, but in gardening terms it usually applies to non-woody plants that live for two or more years. Many tender or short-lived perennials are grown as annuals or biennials, e.g. foxgloves, hollyhocks and wallflowers.

Many perennials are herbaceous, which means that they die down to ground level during winter and re-grow from the base each spring. The disadvantage of this for the gardener is that they can look boring for a considerable part of the year. Herbaceous borders (i.e. borders made up of only herbaceous perennials) will look stunning from mid-spring until autumn, but can look very bleak during the winter. Some plants have interesting seed-heads, e.g. poppies and honesty, but more die down or collapse and just look sad. The way to get round this mid-winter drabness is to plant a mixed border that also includes shrubs, bulbs and annuals to create some colour and interest during the perennials' dormant period.

Perennials are fairly labour intensive, but most are easy to grow and do give good results in return for your efforts. They should be planted in early to mid-spring in good soil. Because they re-grow each year, they need strong root systems, which in turn need rich soils so you should add compost at planting time and mulch well each spring. During the summer months many perennials, like lupins and some campanulas, will need staking and most will need deadheading to prolong the flowering season. In the autumn most should be cut back to just above ground level and tender plants should have their crowns covered with a layer of dry leaves, straw or bark to protect them from frost. Make sure the covering is not too thick, otherwise it will hamper ventilation. The following spring new growth will appear and any dead parts should be cut away. Every three or four years many

perennials such as lupins make an impressive display with buttercups planted in between

plants benefit from being dug up and divided. Plants such as geraniums grow outwards from the centre and this tends to make the centre part less productive as the plant grows. You can dig the plant up, gently remove the old centre and split the rest to form new plants. On the plus side, perennials flower the first year they are planted, most will provide a good display for several months and financially they work out much more economical than annuals as they do not have to be replaced each year.

Scented perennials

Cosmos
Dianthus (Pinks)
Geranium (Cranesbill)
Iris
Lupinus (Lupin)
Monarda (Bergamot)
Nepeta (Catmint)
Phlox
Viola odorata (Violet)
Most herbs e.g. sage, thyme, mint

Grasses

The term 'grass' usually includes sedges, rushes and cats'-tails which are not true grasses. Surprisingly, bamboos are. True grasses have hollow cylindrical stems and flat leaves. Sedges have solid leaves and stems that are triangular if you cut them across and rushes have flat or cylindrical leaves that grow directly out of the ground. Cats'-tails are better known as bulrushes.

All the above can be grown as individual specimens or in a border with perennials and shrubs. Most are very easy to grow but do need an airy site. Sedges need rich damp soil and like some shade, but grasses prefer poor soil and sunlight. If your soil is rich, it is best to dig in some grit or sand before planting. Grasses will survive in light shade but they stand more upright in sunlight. It is important that they are planted in a fairly open position as one of the main attractions of grasses is the way they move in the breeze. Many true grasses are drought tolerant and, once established, will need little watering.

Although grasses do not often have brilliantly coloured flowers, the foliage can be bright varying from brown and greens through to the bright reds of Japanese blood grass (*Imperata cylindrica* 'Rubra'). The foliage itself can be fine and delicate or flat and stiff and grasses vary in height from 15 cm (6 in) to over 4 m (12 ft).

Grasses are a mixture of annuals and perennials. They spread by seed and you need to be careful that some of the more vigorous annual grasses do not turn into weeds. *Briza maxima* (Greater quaking grass or Pearl grass) and *Hordeum jubatum* (Foxtail barley, Squirrel tail grass) can both take over so their flowers need to be deadheaded regularly. Many of the perennials such as *Miscanthus sinensis* (Eulalia grass), *Molinia caerulea* (Moor grass) and *Panicum virgatum* (Switch grass) have attractive seedheads that can be left on over the winter and cut back in spring.

The flowers on grasses are usually small but are often very abundant and can form an impressive display, e.g. *Miscantus*, *Molinia*, *Panicum* and *Pennisetum*. Many grasses also change colour with the seasons, e.g. *Phalaris arundinacae* var *picta* 'Feesey' has green and white leaves that are an attractive pink in spring.

Bamboos

These are woody grasses and can range in size from 30 cm (12 in) to 20 m (70 ft). They are sometimes invasive but you can control their size by regularly mowing round the plant. Alternatively you can restrict their roots by digging a trench 30 cm (1 ft) from the base and deep enough to reach below the level of the roots. Fill this with an impenetrable layer (sheet metal, polythene or concrete) which will contain the roots and restrict their growth. Most like well-drained soil and should only need watering in their first season while they get established. Old stems at the centre can be removed in the spring. If the plant gets too big, simply cut away the excess growth. A selection of bamboos is given below. Make sure you choose one that is the correct size for your garden.

Type	Height	Spread
Chusquea culeou (Chilean bamboo)	4 m (13 ft)	1 m (3 ft)
Phyllostachys aurea (Fishpole bamboo)	4 m (13 ft)	1.5 m (5 ft)
P. Nigra (Black bamboo)	3 m (10 ft)	1 m (3 ft)
Pleioblastus auricomus	1.2 m (4 ft)	60 cm (2 ft)
Sasa palmata – likes shade	3 m (10 ft)	1.5 m (5 ft)
Semiarundinaria fatuosa	5 m (16 ft)	60 cm (2 ft)

Grasses

(Need well-drained soil and full sun.)

Arundo donax (Giant reed, Provencal reed)
Cortaderia (Pampas grass)
Festuca glauca (Blue fescue)
Hakonechloa macra (Hakone grass) – needs shade
Helictotrichon sempervirzens (Blue oat grass)
Miscanthus sinensis (Eulalia grass)
Molinia caerulea (Moor grass) – needs shade
Panicum virgatum (Switch grass)
Pennisetum alopecuroides (Fountain grass)
Phalaris aruninaceae (Gardener's garters, Reed canary grass, Ribbon grass)
Stipa gigantica (Gold oats, Spanish oat grass)

Sedges

Carex (Need moist soil in sun or shade.)
C. comans

C. elata 'Aurea'
C. pendula
C. riparia 'Variegata'

Rushes

(Need moist or wet soil in full sun.)

Juncus effusus 'Spiralis' (Curly rush)
J. inflexus 'Afro' (Corkscrew hard rush)
Luzula sylvatica (Common woodrush) – needs shade

Cats'-tails

(Need moist soil and sun.)

Typha angustifolia (Lesser bulrush)
T. latifolia
T. minima (Dwarf reedmace)

tulips and pansies can be planted together and both come in a wide range of colours

Bulbs

Type	Planting	Flowering	Notes
Allium	Early to mid-autumn	Summer	
Alstromeria (Peruvian lily)	Early spring	Summer	
Anenome blanda	Early autumn	Spring	
Chionodoxa (Glory-of-the-snow)	Early autumn	Spring	
Convallaria majalis (Lily of the valley)	Mid-autumn–winter	Mid late spring	Scented
Crocosmia (Montbretia)	Early spring	Summer	Likes full sun
Crocus (Winter)	Early–mid-autumn	Winter	
Crocus (Spring)	Early–mid-autumn	Early spring	
Crocus (Autumn)	Mid-summer	Early–mid-autumn	
Cyclamen	Late summer/early autumn	Any time depending on species	Needs shade
Dahlia	Spring	Late summer	
Freesia	Mid-spring	Late summer	Scented
Fritillaria	Early–late autumn	Spring	Likes damp conditions
Gallanthus (Snowdrop)	Early–late autumn	Mid–late winter	
Gladiolus	Spring	Summer	Likes sun
Hyacinthoides hyspanica (Spanish bluebell) also *Scilla campanulata*	Early autumn	Spring	Scented
H. non scripta (English bluebell)	Early autumn	Spring	Scented
Hyacinthus	Early–mid-autumn	Spring	Scented
Iris reticulata	Early–mid-autumn	Late winter/early spring	
I. juno	Early–mid-autumn	Spring	
I. xiphium	Early–mid-autumn	Summer	
Lilium	Autumn	Summer	Scented
Muscari (Grape-hyacinth)	Early–mid-autumn	Mid–late spring	
Narcissus (Daffodil)	Early autumn	Spring	Scented
Nerine	Autumn	Following autumn	Protect crowns in winter
Trillium (Wake-robin)	Early autumn	Spring	Woodland
Tulipa	Late autumn/early winter	Late spring	

Apart from one or two shrubs, bulbs provide the earliest colour in the garden and in the autumn they can fill in the gaps left by early perennials or annuals.

This group also includes corms, tubers and rhizomes which grow in a similar way to bulbs. Bulbs are made up of tightly packed fleshy leaves and mostly look like onions e.g. daffodils, tulips and lilies. Corms re-grow from the base of the stem each year and include crocuses and gladioli. Tubers are roots that have swollen so that they can store the necessary nutrients for the flower, e.g. orchids, corydalis and cyclamen. The final group, rhizomes, are actually swollen underground stems that store nutrients and spread out horizontally, e.g. irises.

All bulbs store the nutrition they need within themselves. This is taken in from sunlight through the leaves after flowering so it is very important that you do not cut the foliage back when the flowers are over. Since the leaves have to be left to wither naturally, it is often best to grow bulbs through something, either grass, low-growing perennials or under shrubs whose growth will hide the unsightly stems.

Most bulbs need good drainage and a certain amount of sunshine – cyclamen are about the only ones that will do well in the deep shade under evergreens. Apart from providing these needs, the most important thing is to plant the bulbs at the correct time. As a rough guide most need about six months in the soil before they flower but you need to be careful with tulips as if you plant them too early (i.e. before late autumn or early winter) they will grow too soon and be damaged by late winter frosts. Below is a list of the most common bulbs and their particular features.

Annuals and biennials

Annuals and biennials are plants that complete their entire life cycles in one or two years and are invaluable for providing colour in a new garden and for filling in any gaps in established beds. Some will grow extremely large (up to 2 m/6 ft) and are very useful but do need to be given sufficient space – examples are scotch thistle, sunflower, mullein, larkspur and nasturtium. They are also ideal for container planting as they can be used in seasonal schemes to create year-round colour and interest. They are often referred to as bedding plants as they are usually grown from seed in greenhouses or nursery beds and then moved to their final positions as small plants.

Annuals do everything in one year – in other words they germinate, grow, flower, set seed and die within 12 months, often much less. They can produce a brilliant display of colour but do need good soil, weeding, watering, feeding and regular deadheading in order to be able to do this. Many will then self-seed and come up again in subsequent years. They are divided into two groups according to their hardiness.

Hardy plants will survive frost and can be sown directly outside where they will flower. Many, such as forget-me-not, love-in-a-mist and poppies, do best if sown the previous autumn.

Half-hardy plants cannot be planted out until the risk of frost has passed. Most also need a temperature of 10 °C (50 °F) to germinate. For this reason they tend to be grown under glass, but many are easily available to buy as young plants. One important point to be aware of is that they are frequently put on display for sale before it is warm enough to plant them out. Many may be kept outside during the day but moved to a sheltered spot at night. Do not buy them until you are absolutely certain there is no risk of frost.

Most annuals need full sun and although some will survive in partial shade, only Busy Lizzies and tobacco plants will do well in deep shade.

Biennials establish their roots and leaves in the first year, then flower and set seed in the second. Most should be sown in a nursery bed out of the way in late spring or early summer and moved to their flowering position in mid autumn.

Annuals and biennials are often sold in trays or strips and unless you are going to grow them from seed this is usually the most economical way to buy the plants. Although they tend to be smaller they will quickly grow once planted out. If possible always buy plants that are in bud rather than full flower and always make sure that *all* the plants in the tray are healthy – weaklings are unlikely to recover in time to put on a good display.

Below are lists of plants that are usually grown as annuals or biennials. In fact some, such as *Nicotiana* and *Bellis perennis*, are actually perennials, but usually do better if grown as annuals. If you live in a mild area, you may find many of these plants will have a longer lifespan.

Annuals

S. = sun, Sh. = tolerant of partial shade, Sc. = scented, H. = hardy, HH. = half-hardy

Agrostemma (Corncockle) S. H.
Antirrhinum majus (Snapdragon) S. Sc. HH.
Begonia semperflorens (Begonia) Sh. HH.
Bellis perennis (Daisy) Sh. H.
Calendula officinalis (Pot marigold) Sh. H.
Callistephus chinensis (Aster) S. HH
Centaurea cyanus (Cornflower) Sh. H.
Clarkia S. H.
Consolida ajacis (Larkspur) S. H.
Cosmos bipinnatus S. HH.

Eschscholzia californica (Californian poppy) S. H.
Helianthus annus (Sunflower) S. H.
Heliotropium arborescans (Heliotrope) Sc. HH.
Hesperis matronalis (Sweet Rocket) Sc. H.
Iberis (Candytuft) S. H.
Impatiens (Busy Lizzie) Sh. HH.
Lathyrus odoratus (Sweet pea) S. Sc. H.
Lavatera trimestris (Mallow) Sh. H.
Limnanthes douglasii (Poached egg flower) S. H.
Lobelia erinus S. HH.
Lobularia maritima (Sweet alyssum) S. Sc. H.
Matthiola bicornis (Night-scented stock) Sh. Sc. H.
Nemophila menziesii (Californian bluebell or Baby blue eyes) Sh. H.
Nicotiana (Tobacco plant) Sh. Sc. HH.
Nigella damascena (Love-in-a-mist) Sh. H.
Papaver somniferum (Opium poppy) Sh. H.
Petunia S. HH.
Phlox drumondii (Phlox) S. HH.
Reseda (Mignonette) Sc. H. Sh.
Rudbeckia hirta (Coneflower) Sh. H.
Salvia splendens (Scarlet sage) Sh. HH.

Scabiosa atropurpurea (Scabious) S. H.
Tagetes erecta (African marigold) S. HH.
T. patula (French marigold) S. HH.
Thunbergia alata (Black-eyed Susan) S. HH.
Tropaeolum majis (Nasturtium) S. H.
Verbascum (Mullein) S. H.
Verbena S. Sc. HH.
Zinnia S. HH.

Biennials

Sc. = scented, S. = sun, Sh. = shade

Alcea rosea (Hollyhock) S.
Bellis perennis (Daisy) S.
Dianthus barbatus (Sweet william) S. Sc.
Digitalis purpurea (Foxglove) Sh.
Erysimum cheiri syn *Cheiranthus* (Wallflower) S. Sc.
Lunaria annua (Honesty) Sh.
Myosotis sylvatica (Forget-me-not) Sh.
Oenothera biennis (Common evening primrose) S. Sc.
Onopordum acanthium (Scotch thistle) S.

cosmos is a useful annual as it provides colour in late summer when many perennials and annuals are past their best

vertical elements

The vertical elements of any garden usually fit into one of two categories – either inanimate objects like fences and walls or large plants that provide some kind of vertical structure to the garden like hedges or climbers. The smaller your garden, the greater the impact any vertical element will have. Boundaries are the most important vertical structure in any garden, but trellises and pergolas can also divide the garden up. Remember a boundary marker can always be made into an attractive feature.

At the most basic level, you need some sort of boundary between your land and that of your neighbour. Many properties come with boundary fences, hedges or even walls, but if you do not like what is there you can often, within reason, alter it. Remember that certain properties may have responsibility for the boundary markers and that you may need permission from the relevant authorities if you want to make structural changes.

Boundaries need to be defined but what you put round the edge of your garden can also be used to block unattractive views, create privacy, stop animals or children coming in or going out, provide support for plants and, if necessary, also protection from wind and sun. They will also form the backdrop against which the rest of the garden will be seen. Vertical elements are particularly useful for disguising things. Trellis can support climbers to hide an unattractive fence or shed, shrubs can fill in the gaps of an open fence and hedges can be made interesting by threading climbers, such as roses, clematis or honeysuckle, through them. It is

important to consider what the garden will look like in all seasons – deciduous climbers will only obscure things from view while they are still in leaf.

trellis has many uses and has been used here to give height to the garden and to screen off an unattractive area

Fences and walls

These are probably the most common types of boundary. Most fences are fairly cheap and easy to construct and both fences and walls have the advantage that they do not take up much room – a bushy hedge can easily encroach a metre or so into your garden. One of the best combinations is often fence panels with trellis on top. The fence will give solidity and the trellis on the upper part will provide privacy and support for climbing plants but will not block too much light. If possible, use fence posts that reach the total height of the trellis as this will make the trellis much sturdier and look neater. Fences and walls last a long time so if you are building one from scratch, choose with care. In particular make sure that the style and material is in keeping with the house and garden and that the fence is strong enough to support any climbers you may wish to grow up it. A fence will only be as strong as its upright posts and these should be treated to prevent rot and buried in specialized metal sleeves or in concrete. Walls should have good foundations, a damp course at the base and coping along the top to prevent erosion by rain.

If you want your fence to be a barrier against a strong prevailing wind, it should not be completely solid as this will simply push the wind over the top and possibly create an even worse problem. Ideally 40 per cent should be left open as this will allow the wind through, but slow it down so that it should not do any damage. If you need more privacy than this will provide, you can plant wind-resistant climbers to create an illusion of solidity without blocking the path of the wind totally.

Different types of fences and walls

Type	Description	Advantages	Disadvantages
Post and rail	Vertical posts with two or three horizontal rails attached.	Cheap. Chain link can be added to provide a barrier and support for plants.	No privacy. Does not stop wind or prevent access to property.
Closeboard fencing	Posts with horizontal arris rails and vertical boards nailed to them.	Strong, especially if made out of oak or deal. Suits most styles and works well with trellis.	Expensive. Will not support climbers unless wire or trellis is added.
Lapboard fencing	Machine woven slats made into panels.	Cheap. Easy to put up.	Not particularly attractive. Not as strong as closeboard.
Picket fencing	Arris rails with flat poles nailed, usually at 5 cm/2 in intervals.	Cheap and easy to put up. Especially suitable for cottage styles. Looks good painted.	Does not provide privacy or solid barrier. Will only support small climbers.
Woven hurdles	Panels made of woody stems (hazel or osiers – willow shoots) woven between uprights.	Easy to put up. Good wind channel. Matches plants well and good for climbers.	Not very sturdy unless well fixed to uprights.
Chestnut paling	Halved chestnut stakes held together with wire.	Rolls up. Easy to install. Good temporary measure while waiting for a hedge to grow.	Not very sturdy.
Trellis	Thin batons fixed in square or diamond pattern. Some expands.	Good for increasing height of existing fences. Provides support for climbers.	Can be flimsy. Make sure it is strong enough to support your climber when fully grown.
Walls	Stone or brick.	Long-lasting, attractive. Can be used to link house and garden.	Expensive. Must be well built with good foundations, damp course and coping.
Iron	Metal posts with iron crossbars.	Most suited for front gardens of town houses.	Expensive. Does not provide privacy.
Wire	Wire mesh fixed to vertical posts, usually concrete.	Good support for climbers. Will keep animals in or out. Allows light and wind to pass through.	Can look unattractive. Does not provide privacy. Usually best clothed in climbers.

In terms of maintenance, ideally all fences should be treated annually to prevent rot. In practice, particularly if you have climbers, this is not always possible, but always try to check your fences every spring and autumn to make sure they are in good repair and firmly fixed in the ground.

Hedges

Hedges take up more space than fences or walls, but do provide a very good barrier round your garden and are particularly good at blocking out noise like that of passing traffic. If you are planting a hedge from scratch, the main decisions you need to make are whether you want an evergreen or deciduous hedge and whether you prefer a formal or an informal style. Some hedges, such as hornbeam or beech, have leaves that turn brown in autumn but do not usually drop off, thus providing interesting colour for winter. Informal hedges often take up more room than formally cut evergreens, but many flowering shrubs, like berberis, can make very attractive hedges.

When buying plants for a new hedge, do not be tempted to buy large plants or plant them too close together. Smaller plants (up to 45 cm/18 in) will settle in more quickly and grow faster in the long run. The type of plants you use will determine the ideal spacing to leave between each one, but for most 90 cm/3 ft in between

Different types of hedging

Type	Deciduous (D) or evergreen (E)	Fast or slow	Comments
Berberis darwinii	E	Medium.	Flowers in spring, berries in autumn.
Berberis thunbergii	D	Medium.	Many have interesting leaf colour in autumn.
Buxus sempervirens (Box)	E	Slow.	Good for low hedging.
Carpinus betulus (Hornbeam)	D	Fairly fast.	Leaves change colour but do not drop. Clay soil.
Chamaecyparis lawsoniana (Lawson cypress)	E	Fairly fast on moist soil, slow on chalk.	Be careful to choose the correct size – cultivars range from dwarf to 35 m/120 ft.
Corylus avellana (Hazel)	D	Fairly fast.	Best in large gardens. Can be pruned to control size. Catkins in early spring.
x *cypressocyparis leylandii* (Leyland cypress)	E	Very, very fast.	Needs a minimum height and spread of 2.5 m/8 ft. Can reach 23 m/75 ft.
Fagus sylvatica (Beech)	D	Fairly fast. Chalky soil.	Leaves turn brown, but do not drop. Good windbreak.
Ilex aquifolium (Holly)	E	Slow, but any soil.	Variegated leaves and berries can provide interest. Plant male and female plants.
Lavendula (Lavender)	E	Low-growing only.	Needs full sun. Do not prune into old wood.
Ligustrum (Privet)	E	Fast. Any soil.	Prune twice a year.
Lonicera nitida (Chinese honeysuckle)	E	Fast.	Small flowers followed by berries.
Prunus (Laurel)	E	Fast or fairly fast.	*P. laurocerasus* (Cherry Laurel) or *P. lusitanica* (Portuguese Laurel). Both large.
Pyracantha (Firethorn)	E	Fast.	Berries in winter. Spiny stems. Suitable for exposed site.
Quercus ilex (Holm oak)	E	Slow.	Large, imposing hedge. Good windbreak.
Taxus baccata (Yew)	E	Very slow.	Good dense hedge, can be kept narrow.
Thuja plicata (Western red cedar)	E	Fast.	Will survive in shade and on chalk.

The above chart is only a small selection of the plants which can be used to make hedges: *Cotoneaster, Crataegus* (Hawthorn), *Eleagnus, Escallonia, Euonymus japonicus, Osmanthus x burkwoodii, Rosmarinus officinalis* (Rosemary), *Rosa* (roses, especially *R. rugosa*) and *Spirea* are all suitable for informal hedges).

each plant will allow them to grow properly. Most hedges do best if planted in early winter so their roots can get properly established before they need to provide for new growth in spring.

Until they are established (at least three years depending on the type of hedge) you will need to water your hedge and you should keep the ground at the base free of weeds so the plants do not have to fight for nutrients and water. Once established, the only maintenance your hedge will need is pruning. You will probably have to trim it at least once a year and possibly more if the plant is very fast-growing or you want to train it into a particular shape. Details on this subject are covered in the pruning section.

Climbers

The term 'climbers' covers a huge range of plants, both evergreen and deciduous. Some, such as ivy, are self-clinging and need no support, while others such as jasmine twine themselves around the supports. Clematis and many others hold on with small tendrils. Several non-climbing shrubs can be trained to climb to a certain height by a combination of tying in and pruning. Most climbers are shrubs but there is a group of climbing annuals that are very useful, particularly if you need a climber to fill in a gap temporarily while a slower one grows up. There is a climber to suit most requirements and sites so it is worth taking a little time to consider the possibilities before you make your choice. The list on p. 47 gives the main characteristics of the easiest and most useful climbers. Roses are covered in a separate section on p. 36.

Obvious though it may seem, all climbers need something to climb up, otherwise they will simply turn into ground-cover plants. It is much better to fix the structure to be climbed in place first and then plant suitable climbers round it. You must ensure that any structure will be strong enough to support the plant when it is fully grown. wisterias, *Solanum crispum* (Chilean potato plant) and climbing *Hydrangeas* all eventually develop large, thick and heavy stems that need very sturdy support. Wire netting can be fixed to walls or fences using u-staples. Trellis can also be fixed to walls or fences or placed above them. Position the trellis with the vertical batons next to the wall and the horizontal ones in front so that you can fix the plant ties to them. If you want a more open framework, you can put in vine eyes (nails with loops at their heads) at intervals and thread wire between them.

Always use galvanized fixings that will not rust.

When choosing a flowering climber, take into account the colour of the wall or backdrop. For example, white flowers will not stand out against a white wall, whereas a deep-coloured clematis would look stunning with a white background. You also need to choose carefully if you are planting more than one climber in an area. If possible you should try to stagger the flowering or fruiting times in order to get as long a period of interest as possible. Take into consideration also the pruning times – it is very difficult to prune a climber if it is intertwined with another plant that is just coming into flower. Climbers can also be trained through shrubs, hedges and trees to provide extra interest.

Climbers vary considerably in the density of cover they provide. Jasmines can be trained to twine neatly along a trellis, whereas honeysuckle will grow in a sprawling mass – both can look good but you do need to consider how much space your climber will take up, particularly if you only have a small patio. If you wish to restrict the growth of a climber, you can always plant it in a large container, but remember you will need to devote that much more time to looking after it and ensuring it has enough water and nutrients, even during the winter. Most climbers, in fact, need more care and attention than shrubs. As they are often planted at the base of fences, walls or hedges, they may be in a rain shadow and will need regular watering. You should try to put any plant 45 cm/18 in away from a wall as the bricks will absorb moisture from the soil thereby depriving the plant. Climbers also need regular maintenance to ensure they grow as you want them to. This will involve staking, tying in, feeding, watering and pruning.

The chart opposite shows the requirements and benefits of each plant to help you choose the best ones for your particular garden.

The following shrubs can easily be trained as climbers: *Ceanothus, Chaenomeles* (Quince), *Cotoneaster, Euonymus, Forsythia, Pyracantha.*

Climbing annuals

Cobaea scandens (Cup-and-saucer plant)
Ipomoea (Morning glory)
Lathyrus odoratus (Sweet pea)
Tropaeolum majis (Nasturtium)
Runner beans

Climbing shrubs

Plant	Sun/shade Soil	Time of interest	Comments E: Evergreen D: Deciduous
Actinidia kolomikta	Sun.	Small flowers in summer.	D. Green leaves with cream and red tips.
Akebia	Sun/shade.	Flowers early summer.	Semi E. Fruits may follow in summer.
Campsis (Trumpet vine)	Sun/shade.	Seeds and leaf colour in autumn.	D. Small green flowers in summer. Seed capsules with bright-red seeds.
Clematis I (Virgin's bower)	Sun.	Winter/spring.	E. Needs sunny sheltered wall. *C. armandii*, *C. cirrhosa*, *C. forsteri*, *C. paniculata*.
Clematis II	Sun/shade.	Mid–late spring.	D. Hardier than I. *C. alpina*, *C. macropetala*, *C. montana*.
Clematis III	Roots in shade, stems in sun is best, but not vital.	Early summer.	D. Large-flowered hybrids, e.g. Barbara Jackman, Lasurstern, Lord Neville, Marie Boisselot, Mrs N. Thompson, Nelly Moser, Niobe, The President.
Clematis IV	As above.	Late summer.	Large-flowering hybrids, e.g. Comtesse de Bouchard, Ernest Markham, Hagley Hibrid, Ville de Lyon, Jackmanii.
Clematis V	Sun/shade.	Late summer–mid-autumn.	D. *C. viticella*. Medium-sized flowers. Often tougher and easier than large-flowered hybrids.
Clematis VI	Sun/shade.	Late summer, early autumn.	D. Lantern-shaped yellow flowers (in the *orientalis* group). Good seedheads. *C. tangutica* and 'Bill Mackenzie'.
Fallopia baldschuanica (Russian vine)	Sun/shade.	Mid–late summer.	D. Also *F. auberti* and *Polygonum baldschuanica*. Also known as mile-a-minute. *Very* rampant.
Hedera (Ivy)	Sun/shade.	All year greenery.	E. Self-clinging. Will grow anywhere. Leaf size and colouring varies. The larger the leaf the faster it grows. Variegated leaves need some light.
Hydrangea petiolaris (*Anomala* ssp. *Petiolaris*)	Shade.	Summer.	D. Slow to start but after two to three years will grow huge. Self-clinging.
Jasminum nudiflorum (Winter jasmine)	Shade.	Winter.	D. Good in an exposed site. Yellow flowers appear on bare stems.
Jasminum officinale (Summer jasmine)	Sun/part shade.	Summer–early autumn.	D. Fragrant flowers. Not as tough as *J. nudiflorum*. Needs sheltered site.
Lathyrus latifolius (Perennial pea)	Sun/part shade.	Summer.	Purple flowers, not scented. Also *L. grandifolia*. Stems should be cut to ground level in autumn.
Lonicera (Honeysuckle)	Sun/part shade.	Summer–autumn.	Semi E. Scrambles rather than climbs neatly. Some are very fragrant.
Parthenocissus (Virginia creeper)	Sun/shade.	Autumn.	D. Red leaf colour in autumn. Self-clinging, but needs support at first.
Solanum cripsum (Chilean potato vine)	Sun.	Summer–autumn.	Semi E. Scrambles rather than climbs. *S.c.* Glasnevin is the hardiest.
Tropaeolum speciosum (Scottish flame flower)	Sun.	Mid–late summer.	Perennial. Red flowers, can be followed by blue berries in autumn.
Vitis coigetiae (Ornamental vine)	Sun/shade. Best in poor soil.	Autumn.	D. Huge leaves that turn gold and then red.
Vitis vinifera (Grape vine)	Sun.	Summer–autumn.	D. Small flowers in late spring followed by fruits that can be eaten depending on the climate.
Wisteria	Sun.	Early summer.	D. May remain dormant for several months after planting and must be pruned properly in order to flower well.

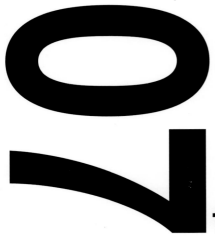 **techniques**

Described below are various techniques that you will find useful, if not essential, when you start gardening. Although these instructions may seem daunting, in practice plants and gardens are fairly forgiving so do not worry too much about doing something at exactly the right time or in precisely the right way. It is important simply to follow the general guidelines and to give your plants the best possible care that you can manage. In the long run, many of these techniques should make life much easier for you – for example, mulching your garden should make weeding unnecessary, cut down on the amount of watering you have to do and enrich your soil into the bargain.

Preparing the soil

Before you can put any plants into the ground it may be necessary to prepare the soil first. The amount of work you have to do will depend on the state of your garden, but most unplanted areas benefit from being dug over before you begin to plant anything. As explained in Chapter 2, you may need to clear the area before you can even get to the soil, but once you have reached it you can start creating *your* garden.

What follows may sound surprising, but you should regard the soil as the most important element in your garden even if it is the most boring to look at. An ideal soil has a deep layer of topsoil with organic matter evenly distributed. It retains moisture but does not become waterlogged, has no large stones and is light and easy to work.

Very few gardens have an ideal combination but most soils can, fairly easily, be improved. The design of the garden largely depends on you, but the quality of the plants largely depends on the condition of the soil. Most plants grow better if they can send their roots down deeply – 45–60 cm (18–24 in) is quite common even for small plants. This anchors the plant securely, gives it access to nutrients in the soil and makes it less susceptible to drought.

Traditionally digging has been regarded as the best way to improve the soil quality and although there is a no-dig method (see p. 50) for most people and gardens digging is the best option because it breaks up the soil, thus allowing roots to grow and water and food to spread

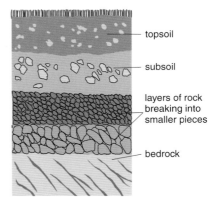

topsoil

subsoil

layers of rock breaking into smaller pieces

bedrock

cross-section of soil, showing turf on top, then topsoil and below that subsoil, with the pieces of rock getting larger towards the bedrock

through and drain away at the correct rate. When you dig you can also mix in food and compost and though this can be done via the surface, it usually spreads better through the soil if dug in. Nutrients that are missing can also be added back into the soil. Care should be taken, however, over when exactly to do this – for example, if lime is added at the same time as fertilizer, the two combine and release harmful ammonia into the soil.

Digging may seem a simple operation but there is a correct way to do it and if you use a spade properly you will find the job is easier and you run less risk of damaging your back. The most important fact to remember is to dig as vertically as possible, i.e. keep your back straight, bend your knees and push the spade straight down rather than at an angle. Place one foot on the top of the blade and push down on it using the weight of your body. Pushing with your arms on the handle will achieve less and give you backache sooner. To lift the soil, use your bodyweight to push the handle down thereby raising the blade with the soil on it. As the handle gets lower, bend your knees rather than your back.

Digging is not something that you have to do very often. In fact once the plants are in place you should not dig to any great extent as it will disturb the plants' roots. Fruit and vegetable plots need regular digging in between crops, but for all other types of gardening the only time you will have to dig seriously is when you are cultivating an area for the first time. Traditionally, in many of the great gardens, all perennials were lifted every three years and the bed dug over, but most people would now regard this as excessive and possibly even harmful.

If you are creating a new bed, the soil will almost certainly be compacted. If it is a new house, builders and machinery will have squashed the soil and even if you are converting an area of lawn it will have become compacted during its years beneath the grass. If this is the case, roots will not be able to push their way into the soil, water will be unable to penetrate it or will become trapped in pockets, which is worse, and earthworms, the great soil improvers, will be unable to move about easily and break up the soil.

For most soils, digging is best done in the autumn when it is damp but not waterlogged. If you find the soil is sticking to your boots, it is too wet to dig. Light soils can be dug in autumn or spring, but all other soils should be dug before winter so the clods of earth can be broken

down by the rain and frost. Do not dig when the surface has frost on it as this will then be buried beneath the surface and take longer to thaw out.

If you intend to do a considerable amount of digging it is worth investing in a good spade with a stainless steel blade. It will seem expensive but will be much more efficient to use as it will cut easily through the soil. It will also last much longer than a cheap model. As mentioned in the chapter on tools, work out roughly how much digging you are liable to do and choose the quality of your spade accordingly. If you are only going to use it to plant a few perennials in an already established garden then a cheaper spade will do the job adequately.

If you are digging in an area with a lot of large stones, such as hardcore, you may need a fork to get through the soil, but wherever possible use a spade as the aim of digging is to move the soil, not just break it up. Forks are useful, however, for digging up roots in their entirety whereas a spade will frequently cut through the root and split it.

For large areas using a Rotavator may seem an attractive option as it will quickly turn over a large area of soil and give what appears to be very impressive results for little effort. The snags are that it will not dig as deep as a spade and if there are perennial weeds it will chop up the roots and spread them around rather than destroy them.

There are two types of digging – single and double. For most situations single is all the garden will need.

depth of trench for single digging

Single digging

Small areas of ground can be simply dug over, but the single digging system of trenches allows larger areas to be dug methodically. If you simply dig at random, it is all too easy to miss out some areas and dig others twice.

First, dig a trench across the area roughly one spade blade (spit) deep and one spade wide.

Put the soil from this trench into a barrow and spread it out along the far end of the area to be dug. It will be used to fill the last trench you dig. Move along from the first trench and dig a similar trench alongside using the soil from the second trench to fill the first. As you do this, pick out any roots of perennial weeds that are exposed. A generous amount of organic material should be mixed in with the soil as you move it into the trench, ideally spread evenly between the surface and the bottom of the trench as this encourages the plant roots to grow downwards.

If you do not want to make your own compost, garden manure can easily be bought from garden centres. While mixing this in, be careful not to tread on soil you have already dug as you do not want to re-compact it. A plank

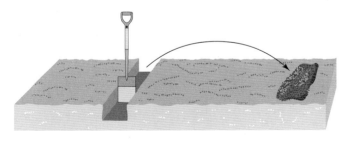

method for single digging: the soil is moved from the first trench to the end of the site where it will eventually be used to infill the last trench

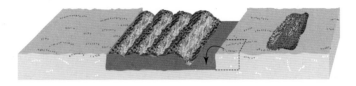

as you work across the site, the soil from each new trench is used to infill the previous one

of wood is often useful to stand on as it will distribute your weight evenly.

Move across the plot repeating this procedure until you reach the far side when you can fill the last trench with the soil that came from the first one. The level of the soil will have risen considerably but this will gradually sink back down as the soil settles. It is not necessary to break up all the clods of earth as the rain and frost of winter will do it for you. Even if the surface appears fairly fine you should always allow at least three weeks between digging and planting or sowing to allow the soil time to sink down.

Ideally the soil should then be left over the winter to be naturally broken down. However much the soil breaks up, when you are ready to plant or sow, you will still need to level it. If possible, this should be done on a day when the soil is dry on top and moist underneath. Push a rake back and forth across the soil, being careful not to dig it into the soil too deeply. If you push away harder than you pull towards yourself, the soil will end up level and the surface debris, such as leaves and twigs, will be caught up in the rake and can easily be cleared away. If you then work across the plot at right angles, it will level out completely and be ready for planting.

No-dig method

There is an alternative system whereby you can improve the condition of the soil without having to resort to digging. Advocates of this system say that digging is actually harmful to the soil as it disrupts the structure. Also turning the soil over can cause it to dry out more quickly and may expose weed seeds which will then germinate. The argument is that in the wild plants grow perfectly well without soil being dug and that any treatment necessary can be applied to the surface. This argument is fine as far as it goes but the problem is that by their very nature gardens are not usually in a very 'natural' state. The soil may be in such poor condition that it is simply not able to respond to this sort of treatment; for example, the heavy machinery involved in building a house might have totally ruined the structure of the soil in the garden. Even in an established garden the soil is rarely in its natural condition as it might well have become compacted under paths or over-cultivated.

If the soil has never been compacted, simply adding organic material to the surface is a perfectly good way to enrich any soil, even heavy clay. It is slow, though, and can look unattractive until the plants grow up. The two main points to remember are that at least 15 cm (6 in) of organic material should be added to the surface every year and that you must *never* walk on the soil. This makes the system particularly suitable for fruit and vegetables where you can put walkways in between the rows or beds.

First you must hoe the surface and pull up any weeds. At this stage you also need to create paths so that you do not have to tread on the growing area. These can be properly laid paths, like bricks or paving slabs embedded in the soil, or simply trampled paths. Bear in mind that although the last option is the easiest it will also become the muddiest, and although straw or bark can be put down to walk on, this will need to be regularly replaced as it sinks into the mud. If you do not want to go to the bother of laying a path, the easiest option is a series of paving stones, large enough to stand or kneel on, placed at regular intervals between the planted areas.

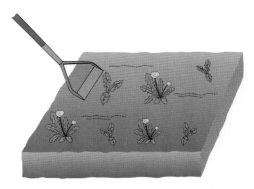

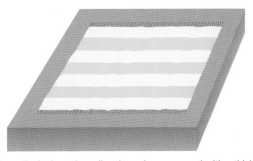

the no-dig method where the soil and weeds are covered with a thick layer of mulch or a solid layer such as carpeting or polythene

Having cleared the area of weeds, you then need to cover it so that no light can get through and allow more weeds to grow. This covering can consist of a thick layer of mulch, black plastic or even old carpeting or cardboard. Ideally this should now be left for up to a year to ensure all weeds are eradicated. Obviously this is not a particularly attractive option but an alternative is to lay down a 10-cm (4-in) layer of organic mulch and pull up any weeds as they appear. This should be left in place for one season, but it is possible to grow certain crops through it such as Brussels sprouts, broccoli or squashes. If you use a porous covering for the soil, such as carpet, newspapers or cardboard, you can cut holes in it to grow plants through.

A specially made black plastic is another option that will allow water through but will block the light and prevent weeds growing.

Once the weeds have been eradicated, other plants can be put in or seeds sown. When you do this, add more mulch as this will keep the soil soft and allow the roots to penetrate down. When planting seedlings, always clear an area around each plant to prevent it rotting.

The arguments for and against digging can be summarized as follows: digging breaks up badly compacted soils and can quickly improve poor quality ones; on the other hand it is hard work, can destroy the soil's structure, turn up weeds and is not a process that occurs naturally. The chances are that the state of your garden will decide the method you need to use. If it is in reasonable condition you will have the option of either method, but if it is badly compacted you will simply have to dig.

Where to buy your plants

Having prepared your garden and decided what you want, you can now go and buy the plants. There are various places where you can find the plants you want.

Specialist nurseries and mail order

This is the place to go if you want a particular variety of plant or if you are buying a major feature for your garden, such as a tree. Many nurseries offer mail order services so you can study their catalogues in the peace and quiet of your home. It is obviously best if you can go and choose the plants yourself, but if you buy from a reputable nursery by mail order the quality of the plants should be good. The main snag about mail order is that you have no precise control over when the plants arrive. Plants do need to be dealt with the minute they come, even if you only roughly heel them in on a spare patch of soil. The main advantages of mail order are that you have a very wide range of plants to choose from and the plants themselves are normally comparatively cheap. Mail order companies and nurseries frequently sell an even greater variety of plants in seed form and some sell plantlets or plugs that you can buy in the spring. This is a particularly good way to buy plants that are hard to germinate.

Garden centres

This is the most convenient and undoubtedly the most popular place to get your plants. Plants are normally well displayed, clearly arranged and you can take them home then and there. A quick look round the garden centre will give you a good idea of the quality of the plants on sale. A well-organized establishment with well-watered, healthy-looking plants will probably give you good value for your money. You will not, however, find many specialized plants in your average garden centre and it is quite an expensive way of buying plants.

Flower shows

Flower shows can be excellent and interesting places to buy plants. Most of the growers are experts and able to offer good advice. You can usually buy the plants on the spot, but if this is not possible you can always order them. The prices do tend to vary enormously although the quality is usually very good.

DIY and hardware shops

There is usually only a limited choice available in these shops and the plants are not necessarily in good condition. Unless you are confident that the plants have been well cared for, it is probably safest only to buy your bedding plants from such outlets.

Market stalls

Again, these stock a limited range of plants but they are usually cheap. A good place to buy annuals and sometimes perennials and small shrubs, but check that the plants look in good condition before you buy them.

What to look out for when buying plants

Having decided where to buy your plants, you then need to know what to look for. Shrubs and trees are available in two main conditions, referred to as bare-rooted or container-grown.

Mail order plants are normally sent out bare-rooted and many shrubs, particularly roses, do well when transported and then planted out in this state. If choosing a bare-rooted plant in a nursery, make sure it is dormant, i.e. no buds are open, the stems look healthy and the roots look strong with no small white roots growing.

The main advantage of container-grown plants is that you can plant them at almost any time of the year. There are a number of points to check out before you buy your plants. Always make sure the compost is damp and the plant is firmly in the pot. If you lift the plant by the base of the stem and it comes out of the pot easily, this indicates that the plant has only just been put in the container and is not a good specimen to buy as it is unsettling for it to be planted out so soon after being repotted. Equally, plants with roots poking out of the bottom of the pot should be avoided as this indicates they have been contained too long and have become pot-bound. Check that the plants look healthy – firm green leaves, even growth and plenty of foliage on evergreens are all signs of healthy growth. When choosing a tree or shrub, small is better than large since a young plant will adapt and settle into your garden much more easily. Some plants, especially evergreens, come with their roots and soil wrapped in a ball of hessian or similar material. This usually works well as long as the wrapping has been kept damp and the roots are not growing round in circles inside it.

When buying perennials, follow the general guidelines for shrubs but bear in mind that a lot die down in the winter and may look unprepossessing at the start of spring. With perennials you can buy a single larger plant and then divide it into several smaller ones.

Bulbs should be firm, free of mould and show slight signs of growth at the top.

The main danger with annuals is that many are not frost hardy and must not be planted out too early. Many of those on display in garden centres early in the season are kept partly under cover or are brought in at night. The time to buy half-hardy annuals is when there is no longer a danger of frost and not when there is a public holiday or an enticing display at your local garden centre.

Planting

The most important consideration when planting anything is to make sure it is positioned in a spot where it will be happy. It is a complete waste of time, effort and money to put a sun-loving plant in deepest shade, however much you may want it to grow there. You must also make sure that the eventual size of the plant and its roots will be suitable for your chosen spot. This is particularly important for trees – they should never be planted near buildings because of the spread of their roots.

Timing is also important. Most plants do best if planted during their dormant period so they can concentrate on establishing a good root system before their main growth and flowering period. Autumn and spring are usually the best times, depending on the plant and the condition of the soil. Most small plants do better if moved in the spring and this is also a more suitable time if you have heavy soil that could become waterlogged during the winter. As a rough guideline, hardy deciduous plants should be planted in the autumn in average soils and less hardy and evergreen plants are best planted in the spring. All tender annuals must obviously not be planted out until after the last frost.

Basic planting rules apply to everything:

- The hole for your plant needs to be dug deep and wide enough to allow for the addition of compost round the plants. This will encourage the roots to spread outwards.

- The plant must be fixed firmly in the soil and given plenty of water both before and after planting. Trees and shrubs in particular will need watering throughout the first two years of their lives.

Planting container-grown shrubs

These can be planted at any time but the soil should not be too wet, too dry or frozen.

1. Soak the plant well.

how to plant container-grown shrubs

first water the plant, then check the hole is deep enough

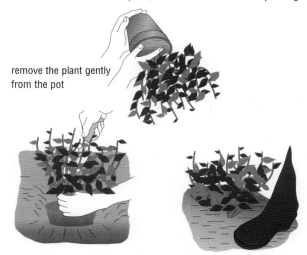

remove the plant gently from the pot

position in the hole, fill gently with soil and compost and finally tread down firmly

2. Dig a hole to the correct depth and double the width of the pot.

3. Mix compost and bonemeal into the soil at the base of the hole.

4. Gently remove the plant from the pot by turning the pot on its side and tapping the sides and the bottom. Never pull a plant out of its container by its stem. Loosen some root ends and put the plant in the hole so that the soil mark on the stem is level with the top of the hole.

5. Fill in with a mixture of soil and compost. Firm into place.

6. Water well and mulch putting a 5-cm (2-in) layer on the ground covered by the spread of the branches as this is a good indicator of the area the roots will cover.

Planting container-grown trees

1. Soak the tree well before planting.

2. Dig a hole one spit deep and 1.20 m (4 ft) across. Then dig a second spit's depth and mix the soil with compost. Also add a fertilizer, such as bonemeal, which is high in phosphates and will encourage the roots to establish.

3. Fix a stake so it is on the windward side of the tree as this will give maximum support. The height of the stake above the ground will depend on the tree, but 90 cm (3 ft) is usually sufficient unless the tree's stem is very flexible. This will allow the tree to develop and strengthen so that after two years it can usually be removed. Use buckle and spacer ties to hold the tree in place and check them regularly to make sure they do not get too tight as the tree grows.

4. Remove the tree from the pot by turning it on its side and tapping the bottom. Never pull a plant out of a container by its stem. Gently loosen the root tips away from the soil to encourage them to grow outwards.

5. Put the tree into the hole ensuring it is straight and fill around it with a mixture of soil and compost, being careful not to leave any air pockets.

6. Firm the tree down well ensuring that the old soil mark on the stem is level with the soil.

7. Mulch and water as before.

8. If you need to add a stake after you have planted the tree, put it in at an angle so you do not damage the roots.

9. After two years shake the tree and if the roots remain firm you can remove the stake. Always do this at the beginning of the growing season so that the tree can gain strength while the climate is mild.

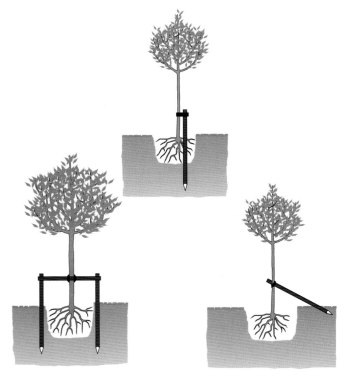

various methods of staking a tree
remember that if the stake will go down between the roots it must be put in place first so the roots can be spread round it and will not be damaged

Planting bare-rooted trees and shrubs

It is vital that the roots should never be allowed to dry out and with this in mind any bare-rooted plants must be planted as soon as possible.

1. Prune any roots that are disproportionately long and remove any damaged ones.

2. Dig a hole large enough to allow the roots to spread out and down when the soil mark on the stem is level with the surface of the soil.

3. Fix the stake in place, as before.

4. Mix bonemeal into the soil at the bottom and, with your tree or shrub in place, gently trowel in a mixture of soil and compost avoiding any air pockets.

5. Fill to the surface and gently firm down. Do not press as hard as you would with a container-grown plant as the roots are more vulnerable.

6. Mulch and water as for container-grown plants.

Planting roses

Bare-rooted roses should be planted between late autumn and early spring. Those in containers can be planted at any time. The planting techniques are roughly the same as for shrubs, but you should mix in plenty of manure and bonemeal at the base of the hole and position the plant so that the joint where the rootstock starts is 2.5 cm (1 in) below the surface. After planting, prune back to two to three buds per stem. This may seem vicious but it will encourage more vigorous growth.

Planting climbers

The soil at the base of a wall is always dry so try to put the plants 30–45 cm (12–18 in) away. Plant as for shrubs. After planting, untie the stems and gently spread them out and train them in the correct directions. Remove all the ties and add new ones, ideally using soft green twine, which will allow for growth.

Planting bulbs

this bulb has been planted at twice its depth, i.e. with twice the height of the bulb between the top of the bulb and surface of the soil

As a rough guideline, bulbs should have twice their own depth of soil above them. Reduce this if your soil is very heavy. Mix sand in at the base of the hole to prevent the bulb from rotting. Embed the roots firmly in this and fill the hole, ensuring no air is trapped. If you are planting a lot of bulbs, a bulb planter makes the job much easier as it digs holes exactly the right shape. For a natural look, scatter the bulbs by hand and plant them where they land. When planting corms, it may not be obvious which way up they should go. Lay them on their sides as this will not do as much damage as planting them upside down.

Planting perennials and annuals

Perennials are usually best planted in spring or autumn and the method is the same as for shrubs. Annuals should be planted in late spring to early summer. Some may need hardening off (see propagation, p. 73) and others cannot be planted until after the last frost. Remember annuals in particular are very delicate when they are being planted out and should always be lifted by the leaves or rootball, not the stem.

If you wish to plant annuals or perennials in between paving stones on a patio, clear out the gaps as much as possible with a trowel or knife. Push compost into the hole first and, after planting, water gently so as not to wash the soil away.

Mulching

Mulch is a layer of matter that you put on top of the soil around plants. It can be organic matter, such as compost or bark, or inorganic, like plastic or gravel and according to what sort of mulch you use it has various functions – preventing the growth of weeds, keeping the soil warm in winter and cool in summer, reducing evaporation and enriching the soil. In some cases it also makes the garden look attractive. No single mulch will do everything, so use the chart on p. 57 to work out what you need and, if necessary, use a combination, e.g. you could dig in manure and then put a layer of bark on top.

To be effective, the mulch must be at least 5 cm (2 in) deep and should be laid down at planting time and thereafter in spring and autumn. The soil should be well prepared beforehand, i.e. weed-free, well nourished and damp. Mulch is usually best applied with a spade, or trowel for smaller plants. This ensures you can spread an even layer over the soil and leave a gap immediately around the stems of plants to stop the damp mulch sitting up against the stems and causing them to rot.

when applying mulch always leave a gap around the stem of the plant so it does not get damp and rot

Making your own compost

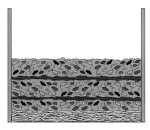

cross-section of homemade compost, showing a layer of fibrous stems at the bottom, then a layer of kitchen refuse, grass and straw and then a thin layer of soil
the general refuse and straw can be repeated to the top of the bin

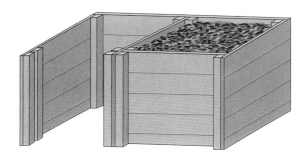

a double bin with removable front panel allows you to use one batch of compost while the other matures

In order to create valuable compost you need to provide a balance of ingredients and a warm, dry place for it to decompose. It is no good simply throwing all your green waste onto a heap and hoping for the best. Wooden or brick-built compost bins with a lid are the most satisfactory as they will keep the warmth in and the damp out. Plastic is not so well insulated. It is important to keep a balance between the layers of green matter or household waste and layers of straw or twigs or even shredded paper that will help the air to circulate. You can also add a 2.5 cm (1 in) layer of soil every 15–30 cm (6–12 in) if you wish which will bulk it up. Turning your compost will encourage it to decompose faster – with one turn in warm weather it should be ready in three months, six in the winter. When you turn the compost you should see little red worms. These are very beneficial and help decomposition. They should appear naturally, but you can also buy them if necessary. All your uncooked kitchen waste can go on the compost heap including tea leaves, coffee ground and eggshells. Annuals weeds are

fine as long as they do not have too many seed heads, but perennials weeds, like couch grass, ground elder and bindweed, should be avoided as they will simply put out roots and start to grow again. Grass cuttings should ideally be mixed in with other matter, otherwise they will form an impenetrable layer that will stop the air circulating. Other points to be aware of are that woody or thorny material will decompose slowly, earthy roots will lower the overall temperature of the compost heap and potato peelings may sprout!

Compost is ready to use when all the separate elements have broken down and it no longer smells. If it, or any manure, is still decomposing, nitrogen may be lost, in the form of ammonia in the case of farmyard manure, and the heat generated by decomposition may damage plants.

Leaves can be added to the general compost heap, but leaf mould is usually better made separately as it takes much longer to decompose. Construct a heap consisting of 15 cm (6 in) of leaves to 2.5 cm (1 in) of soil using fallen autumn leaves. Oak and beech are traditionally considered the best and London plane should be avoided as it takes too long to decompose. The leaf pile should be left for one year and used as a mulch the following autumn.

Feeding plants

If you mulch the soil with compost you will already have provided some of the food your garden needs. It is important to remember that gardeners require plants to put on an unnaturally spectacular display and also to grow in unnatural proximity to other plants. For plants to develop and thrive in this way you must provide them with more food than they would need if growing in the wild. Plants benefit most from food that is supplied during their growing season, i.e. mid-spring to mid-summer. The vast choice of food available means that there is something suitable for every gardener and garden. All foods work better if the soil is damp – dry roots will be too weak to take up nourishment and may be damaged by an intensive dose of plant food.

Organic food

This is of animal or vegetable origin and in the form of mulch is covered on p. 55. It is usually slow-acting and provides food over a long period of time. Bonemeal is the

Types of mulch and their uses

Type	Uses and Nutritional value	Availability	Other
Bark	Little nutritional value. Breaks down slowly. Prevents evaporation. Deters slugs and snails.	Easily available at garden centres.	May be acidic. Very attractive.
Garden compost	Good – depending how balanced it is.	Slow to make and hard to make enough.	Can have weed seeds. Must be well rotted.
Farm Manure	Good. Horse manure is especially useful on clay where the straw in it breaks up the soil as it is incorporated.	Horse manure is usually easier to get than cow and pig manure.	Can have weed seeds. Must be well rotted, i.e. no smell and you cannot see the straw.
Mushroom compost	Good.	Available at more specialized garden centres.	Alkaline so cannot be used round lime-hating plants.
Leaf mould	Good.	Takes one year to make.	Not attractive. Can be acidic.
Cocoa shells	Good.	Can be hard to get.	By-product of chocolate industry. Acidic. Very light, only stable when wet.
Grass	OK but can lose nitrogen during decomposition.	Easily available if you have a lawn.	Can contain weed seeds. Do not use if lawn has been treated with weed killer. Spread thinly to stop it forming a mat. Unattractive.
Seaweed	Good.	Only practical for seaside gardens.	Leave to rot down first or wash off salt and dig in straight away.
Straw and hay	Good barrier between plants and soil. Can be composted for digging in.	Usually only available in large quantities.	Can have weed seeds. Unattractive, especially when wet. Best for temporary uses such as strawberries.
Grit or pebbles	No nutritional value. Prevents water evaporation, stops weeds, slugs and snails.	Expensive and heavy.	Unattractive when the stones and soil start to mix.
Polythene, newspapers, old carpets	No nutritional value. Protects soils and prevents weeds.		Unattractive. See no-dig method on p. 50.

most popular organic food that you can buy. It is particularly effective when added at the time of planting as it is high in phosphates which encourage root growth. Liquid seaweed food is also easily available and very nutritious.

Inorganic food

This is usually fast-acting and can be synthetically produced or developed from minerals that occur naturally in the earth.

All foods contain varying degrees of the three main nutrients (nitrogen, phosphorous and potassium) that plants need to grow. Small amounts of other nutrients, e.g. calcium, iron and zinc, are also needed but these are usually present in sufficient quantities in most soils and should not need to be added unless your plants show signs of stress such as leaf loss or discolouration.

- Nitrogen (N) encourages leaf growth and is particularly useful for grass and leafy vegetables. A deficiency is indicated by weak stems and small leaves.

- Phosphorous (Phosphates/P) is important for most development and is necessary for young plants, root vegetables and fruits. A deficiency is indicated by stunted stems, small purplish leaves and low fruit yield.

- Potassium (Potash/K) helps the plant produce flowers and fruit and is also necessary for potatoes. Deficiency is shown by yellow or brown leaves, a low yield of flowers or fruit and a tendency towards disease.

In practice most fertilizers indicate clearly what they are best used for, so you don't have to worry too much about what they contain. A vast array of foods is available and it is worth asking at your local garden centre for a particular recommendation. The chances are the people who work there will have gardens in the area and will know what is most suitable. Most commercially available foods are compounds, i.e. a mixture of the three elements. Many of the most popular products, such as Growmore, contain equal levels of all three nutrients and are therefore perfectly balanced. Straight foods usually contain only one nutrient and are geared for a particular deficiency. Whatever you are using always be careful to follow the instructions as too much of something can often be as harmful as too little.

Solid food

Granules of solid food can be sprinkled round the base of the plant or put into the soil at the time of planting. Slow-release sticks of fertilizer can be stuck in the soil and animal manure in pellets can be scattered on the surface. Always try to avoid contact with the leaves as they can be scorched.

Liquid foods

These can also include soluble powders and are administered via a watering can or hose attachment. Again avoid too much contact with the leaves.

Foliar feed

This is taken in via the leaves and is frequently included in pesticides to give all round help to the plant. The goodness enters the plants directly through the sap and is particularly useful for sick plants that may not have a strong root system. The plants should be sprayed on still, dry evenings to gain maximum benefit.

Watering

More than food, water is essential for your plants' survival. The amount they need varies enormously, but all plants need some water. Trees and shrubs will need watering for their first two years, perennials for their first year and annuals and vegetables throughout their lives. Plants within 60 cm (2 ft) of a wall, those in containers and shallow-rooted plants, like rhododendrons, will also need constant watering. Exact amounts that you should give are not specified here as there are too many variables, including your soil, the density of your plants and the general climate. Remember that the wind can dry plants out just as much as direct sunshine.

It is important to water before the plants wilt – a good test is to feel how damp the soil is 5 cm (2 in) below the surface. If it is dry you need to water. It is best to water in the evening, but you can water during the day if necessary as long as you avoid watering in hot sunshine. Never aim a strong hose jet directly at the plant as you can easily damage the leaves and wash soil away from around the roots.

It is better to water well shrubs and trees once a week rather than provide a little water every day. Small

a circular ridge of earth round the plant will create a basin in which water can be stored and used by the plant when necessary
the size of the ring should be roughly the same as the leafy area of the plant as this will correspond to the spread of roots below the surface

amounts of water encourage small surface roots, which are more vulnerable than deep-set ones. Containers, especially hanging baskets, and vegetables and annuals cannot last that long without water and may need watering at least once a day during hot weather. If you really dislike watering or are often away from home, choose drought resistant plants or install an irrigation system. These either work on a drip system, whereby spurs come off the main pipe and drip water onto the roots, or by a perforated pipe system, which has small holes that spray water at the plants.

Sprinklers may seem like a good idea, particularly for lawns, but they are very wasteful as much of the water is lost through evaporation.

Water butts are an excellent way of collecting water and can be positioned so the run-off from the gutters flows into them. If using a wooden butt, ensure it is treated and fully waterproof. Always cover the butt with a lid to prevent algae growing and small animals falling in. Purpose-built water butts are available with a pipe in the lid for the water to drain in and a tap further down the side to let it out.

Another way to conserve water is to create shallow depressions round the base of larger plants by building a circular soil wall. This can be filled with water that will drain down to the roots rather than running off and soaking in elsewhere.

Dealing with pests, diseases and weeds

However careful you are, at some time your plants will suffer at the hands of pests, diseases or disorders. Pests are animals or insects that harm plants by eating them or living on them. Diseases are caused by fungus, viruses or bacteria. Disorders result from poor growing conditions, which in turn reduce the plant's resistance to pests and diseases. Disorders are the least common problem you will have to face and on the whole are the easiest to deal with. Many disorders are caused by too much or too little water or by growing plants in the wrong situation or type of soil. If you provide the correct levels of water and ensure the soil is suitable and nutritious you should have few problems in this area.

It is worth facing up to the fact right from the outset that your garden will never be perfect. Most plant problems in the garden result in disfigurement rather than permanent damage and if you try to eliminate all pests and diseases you will turn your garden into a war zone and never be able to relax in it. You also need to decide whether you want to use chemical products or not. You can, of course, adopt a balance of using natural and chemical methods but to a certain extent any chemicals introduced into your garden will upset the natural balance. This may not be immediately apparent and may not even do any great harm but the more we discover about the use of chemicals the more we realize how damaging their effect on the environment is. Many chemicals that were thought to be safe 30 years ago have now been banned and although this means that chemicals in use now tend to be less harmful one can never be sure of their impact. Also some pests just have to be lived with rather than eradicated. If your garden has slugs it will continue to have slugs to some extent regardless of how many slug pellets you put down. You will also probably destroy useful predators at the same time as trying to wipe out the slugs. For many people the best solution is simply to make life uncomfortable for the slugs by putting down sharp mulch and growing plants they do not like. Thus discouraged, perhaps they will move on to someone else's garden!

Whatever method you adopt, prevention rather than cure is the ideal to aim for. If you buy healthy plants, choosing resistant strains where possible, and provide suitable conditions for them, you will give them a better chance of withstanding the onslaught of any pests or diseases. It also helps if you keep your garden as clean and tidy as possible. Clear away heaps of weeds and leaves rather than leaving them to rot near other plants where they can cause rot or disease. It also helps if you deal with any problems as soon as they appear. Keeping on top of pests and diseases may sound like an endless vigil, but don't worry too much – deal with the serious problems and let everything else pretty much take care of itself. It can.

Organic pest and disease control

Organic methods for dealing with problems divide into two areas – first of all trying to get nature on your side by encouraging helpful predators and using companion planting to deter pests and secondly deploying only naturally derived products to deal with any problems that arise. Not all creatures that appear in the garden are a nuisance. Everyone knows that ladybirds eat aphids but so do hoverflies, which look like small wasps, and lacewings. Although birds are pests regarding fruit, they have their uses too as many eat slugs and snails. Incidentally if you do use slug pellets be very careful which you use as some can harm birds if they eat infected slugs. Frogs, toads and shrews are also invaluable helpers, as are hedgehogs. (If lighting a bonfire, always make sure a hedgehog is not hibernating in it.)

Companion planting can help by deterring pests or diseases: nasturtiums keep woolly aphids off apple trees, marigolds (*Tagetes sinuata*) protect potatoes from eelworm, and garlic planted with roses will deter aphids. Lemon basil planted with tomatoes not only deters greenfly but also improves the flavour of the tomatoes. Parsley and chives are both said to prevent blackspot and onions and carrots planted together will reduce both carrot fly and onion thrips.

Various organically approved products are available, which are made from plant or mineral extracts. Pyrethrum and derris are the commonest and are available in powder or liquid form. Pyrethrum is made

Common pests and how to deal with them

Pest	Problem	Cure
Slugs and snails	Will eat anything. Plants most at risk: hostas, clematis, delphiniums, tulips, marigolds, and lupins. Also most young plants and many vegetables.	Sharp mulch or gravel will deter them. Also salt or eggshells. Pellets or liquid treatment are available, but must be reapplied after rain. Resistant plants: shrubs, perennials with spikes or hairy stems and leaves, snapdragons, tobacco plants, heliotrope, some herbs, e.g. rosemary and lavender.
Aphid: green, brown or blackfly	Suck plant sap and can distort growth. The sticky excreta may lead to mould. Plants at risk: roses, honeysuckle, nasturtiums, potatoes, carrots and lettuces.	Small quantities can be picked off. Spray with specialized products or soapy water or infusion of rhubarb leaves. See companion planting on p. 101.
Ants	Farm aphids for the honeydew, which ants like to eat. Can weaken roots with nests and spread disease.	Destroy nests using organic or chemical solution.
Carrot fly	Larvae eat carrots, parsnips and celery.	Plant near onions, avoid thinning and put low screens (60 cm/24 in) around the plants.
Caterpillars	Eat leaves and flowers. Some produce unsightly webbing.	Remove by hand. Not usually serious. They provide food for birds and then turn into butterflies.
Leaf miners	White or brown blisters on leaves containing larvae. Particularly affect chrysanthemums.	Pick off affected leaves.
Moles	Ruin lawns.	Spurge and rue planted round the edge of the lawn will deter moles. Traps or poison can be used.
Birds	Can eat fruit.	Use netting.
Rabbits	Eat young plants.	Put up chicken wire 1 m/3 ft high, one quarter below ground. Put wire collars around all new plants. Rabbit-proof plants: *Aconitum, Anemone, Aster* (Michaelmas daisy), *Astilbe, Buxus* (Box), *Ceanothus, Convallaria, Cotoneaster, Digitalis* (Foxglove), *Euphorbia* (Spurge), *Fuchsia, Geranium* (Cranesbill), *Helleborus, Hemerocallis* (Day lily), *Iris, Kniphofia, Nepeta, Papaver, Paeony, Rosa, Rosmarinus, Sedum, Spirea, Vinca.* Even these plants will be vulnerable when young and should be protected with netting.

Common diseases and how to deal with them

Disease	Symptom	Cure
Black spot	Spots on leaves, especially roses.	Remove leaves and burn. Chemical treatments are available.
Canker	Diseased bark. Appearance varies with plant.	Chemical treatments are available. Prune diseased parts.
Honey fungus	Plant weakens and dies. Black strands grow up stems.	This is a serious problem. Dig up the plant and all its roots and destroy. Sterilize the soil and leave for two years. Then plant resistant varieties – e.g. yew, beech, clematis, ivy or honeysuckle.
Grey mould	Discoloured patches on flowers and grey fluffy growth on flowers first but it may then spread to stems.	Increase ventilation and reduce moisture. Cut away diseased part and remove any debris. Chemicals available.
Powdery mildew	White powder on leaves, which causes them to curl and drop.	Caused by damp air but dry roots. Remove infected parts and ensure only roots are kept damp. Chemical alternative available.
Rust	Small orange or brown patches on both sides of leaves.	Remove leaves, improve ventilation. Chemicals available. Cut mint right back and allow to regrow.
Scab	Brown scab on fruit and leaves, especially attacks apples, pears and pyracantha.	Prune to increase ventilation. Remove infected leaves. Do not store infected fruit. Chemicals available.

from the pyrethrum plant. It is short-lasting in its effects and is only harmful to insects. Unfortunately it is harmful to all insects so you should only use it in the evening when beneficial insects such as bees and ladybirds are no longer flying around. Derris is also derived from plants and although it is not harmful to humans, birds or rodents it is extremely dangerous to fish and tortoises. Soft soap products are also available that are effective against aphids, but do not harm ladybirds or other insects. The effects of most of these products are fairly short-lived so you may need to re-treat the plants at regular intervals.

Chemical treatment of pests, diseases and weeds

Chemicals in the form of garden pesticides are split into three groups – fungicides that fight fungal diseases, herbicides that kill weeds, and insecticides that deal with insects. Always be sure to pick a product that is suitable for your needs and follow the instructions exactly. Insecticides are divided into those which kill the insect on contact, those which coat the leaves of the plant and make them unpalatable and those which are systemic and treat the whole plant by entering the sap. The latter do this via the leaves or roots and any new growth after application should be protected. This type of product is not usually suitable for food plants. Always make sure

the product you are going to use will not harm the plant itself, but only treat the problem. As a general rule avoid spraying young plants or those in flower and if possible spray on still evenings to minimize damage to neighbouring plants. Once you have treated the plant, feed it to help it recover more quickly.

Many other pests may also affect your garden. If the problem looks serious, go to your local nursery with a sample of the affected plant. (This also applies for diseases and deficiencies.) They should be able to provide you with an organic or chemical treatment to deal with the problem.

Weeds

Throughout garden history weeds have been described as plants that are in the wrong place. The problem is that in most gardens, especially small ones, there is no right place for these plants. Most do not look particularly attractive and they all take up space, nutrients and water that could be better supplied to plants you actually want to grow. Weeds are a particular threat to young plants as they are native to the area, have chosen a spot perfect for their needs and will therefore probably be stronger and grow faster than many of the specimens you have planted yourself. Clearing an area of invasive weeds can be very hard work and in some cases disheartening as weeds have a tendency to reappear with alarming speed, but at the other end of the scale pulling up small weeds from an established flowerbed can be a simple and rewarding task.

Weeds can be divided into two groups, annual and perennial, which require slightly different treatment.

Annual weeds
These complete their life cycle within a season and the vital thing is to prevent them from setting seed. An old saying goes that one weed's seeds are seven years' weeding, i.e. if you allow annual weeds to seed you will be dealing with the consequences for seven years. However, annual weeds are not totally bad. Apart from anything else they indicate that the soil is fertile. Most are reasonably easy to pull up, they will enrich the compost heap and if you don't want to dig them up you can just hoe them as they appear.

Perennial weeds
These can be a more serious problem, particularly the invasive ones that will take over your garden if given half a chance. Some spread by seed, but most have large and efficient root systems – if you leave one cm (half an inch) of some roots in the soil the plant will quickly re-grow. In other words, to get rid of perennial weeds you must dig out or destroy the entire plant. If you regularly remove the surface growth you will weaken the plant and reduce the problem but you are unlikely to kill it totally. Perennial plants that you dig up should be burnt and never put on the compost as they will simply establish themselves there. Listed below are the six worst perennial weeds, but don't worry – since weeds only grow in habitats that suit them perfectly you are unlikely to encounter more than one or two in your garden at the same time.

Bindweed (Convulvulus arvensis)
This twines around plants and eventually strangles them. The roots can spread 5 m (15 ft) and the winding stems will grow faster than most garden plants. It only seeds in fine, dry summers but these seeds can lie dormant for up to 30 years!

Ground elder (Aegopodium podagaria)
This has a network of stems just below the ground, which destroy other plants. It has an irritating habit of growing up through garden plants thus making eradication very difficult.

Couch grass (Elymus repens)
Another plant with a creeping root system. This can be dug up quite easily but the fine white roots have a tendency to break off and re-grow.

Dock (Rumex crispus and R. obtusifolius)
This may be useful to soothe the stings of nettles, but it serves no other purpose in the garden. Plants mostly spread by seed and can produce up to 30,000 seeds in a single year.

Horsetail (Equisetum arvense)
The roots usually spread 2–2.5 m (6–8 ft). It is resistant to many chemicals and can often only be eradicated by applying a thick mulch to the area for two to three years.

Japanese knotweed (Polygonum cuspidatum)
This started off as a garden plant but it is so rampant that it is now regarded as a weed. It is hard to control, especially in damp areas where it thrives.

There are, of course, hundreds of other weeds but these six are the greatest threats to your garden.

Methods of weed control
Depending on your strength, patience and inclination there are various ways of dealing with weeds.

Hand pulling seems laborious as it involves getting on your hands and knees and digging the weeds up with a handfork, but it is the best method for weeds found growing in amongst flowerbeds. It is better to do a small area really thoroughly than a large area roughly. This will prevent the weeds from re-growing. Make sure you remove the whole weed and clear away any rubbish straight away, burning or destroying perennial weeds and composting any annuals that do not have seeds.

Hoeing is another relatively easy method of weeding and is particularly useful in vegetable gardens where the plants are growing in straight lines. Using a hoe is explained in Chapter 4, and while hoeing will not get rid of perennial weeds it should reduce the annual ones and will keep your problems under control quite easily. Always make sure the blade is sharp, the soil dry and that you do not put the blade too far below the surface. You must also be careful that you do not inadvertently hoe neighbouring plants.

Digging is a more labour intensive method and is described on p. 48. If you have a bed infested with weeds it is the best approach. First dig up any plants you want to save and wash them under a tap to ensure no weed roots remain, if necessary dividing the plants. Then dig the area over thoroughly with a fork and remove all the roots. Turning the soil will unearth some annual weeds but they will be easy to remove as they appear. The plants can then be put back in the clean soil.

Another alternative for a large garden is to remove the plants and sow rye grass. Leave it for two years keeping the grass short, which should smother most weeds. You can then clear the grass and plant up the bed.

Ground cover plants can be used to suppress weeds although you will need to weed or mulch for the first couple of years while the plants get established. Be careful that they do not grow too rampantly and take over. Remember Japanese knotweed began life as a garden plant.

Some plants will also help you to clear weeds. Potatoes suppress most weeds and can be usefully grown in a bed you want for ornamentals the following year. The roots of *Tagetes minuta*, a type of marigold, are useful as they put out a substance that deters couch grass and ground elder.

Of course some weeds are perfectly acceptable and can be encouraged. Unless you want an immaculate lawn with stripes, daisies look very attractive in amongst the grass and cow parsley by hedges and under trees can be beautiful. Even nettles have their uses as they encourage butterflies. Remember that there is a fine and wavy dividing line between wild flowers and weeds.

Mulching will suppress most weeds providing it is at least 5 cm (2 in) deep, but many mulches contain weed seeds. Solid covering such as black plastic, newspapers or old carpeting weighed down will suppress any growth but it does not look attractive and may take two to three seasons to destroy all perennials completely. If you adopt this method it is possible to disguise the covering by putting a layer of bark on top.

Flame guns may seem a drastic and dangerous approach but can be very successful. The flames burn all the surface weeds and are particularly useful for destroying annuals and their seeds. The downside is that you may have to treat the area several times in one season and that you must obviously be very careful not to destroy or damage surrounding plants.

Chemicals

As with all aspects of gardening there is a whole range of chemicals available to help you deal with weeds. Herbicides have been extensively used in agriculture and commercial gardening for some time but there are now fears that they may do long-term damage to the soil and the environment in general. However, chemicals can be very effective in getting rid of weeds and increasingly you can choose products to deal with specific problems. Chemical herbicides kill so always use them very carefully, follow the instructions exactly, wear protective clothing and do not use in warm weather or on windy days. Herbicides are either selective or non-selective. Selective ones will only target certain weeds, e.g. lawn weedkiller only destroys broad-leaved plants. As their name implies non-selective weedkillers will destroy anything in their path and are best used on uncultivated land.

Contact weedkillers kill greenstuff and are neutralized once they reach the soil. Unfortunately they are usually non-selective and will kill or damage anything they contact. Perennial weeds are rarely killed outright but may be weakened.

Systemic or translocated weedkillers enter the plants via the leaves and are transferred to the root. This is a fairly slow system and may need more than one application. It is a particularly useful method for shrubby weeds such as brambles and ground elder but can be used against all perennials.

Residual herbicides enter the plant via the soil and kill the weeds as they germinate. This method will also harm garden plants and can remain in the soil for more than one season. Because of this it is best only used on paths or patios where you do not want anything to grow. A useful alternative for these situations is salt, which can be sprinkled into the crevices.

Ground cover plants

These can be used to prevent weeds growing, but you will have to weed whilst they are getting established. A full list of ground cover plants is given on p. 82.

Pruning

Many plants in a garden need pruning, not only for their own well-being but also to encourage them to perform in a particular way. Plants in the wild are obviously not pruned, but garden plants frequently need their size or shape restricted and are also often required to produce an unnatural amount of flowers or fruit. The whole subject may seem overwhelming, but there are various simple ground rules and these apply to most plants.

Pruning is the cutting away of parts of a woody plant, i.e. tree or shrub, but it also extends to the deadheading of all flowering plants. The removal of the foliage of some perennials in the autumn is called cutting down rather than pruning.

Pruning is carried out with three main aims:

1. To improve the health or condition of the plant. Dead, diseased or even weak stems should be removed as soon as possible.

2. To improve the shape of the plant. Branches that grow inwards across the centre of the plant should, if possible, be removed. Any tangle in the middle of the plant will reduce the overall ventilation and make the plant more susceptible to disease. Plants that are growing unevenly can be kept in shape by pruning. Topiary, the art of shaping plants, is really a type of intensive pruning. With some plants it is possible to reduce or restrict the overall size by pruning, but beware: pruning can often stimulate growth as the plant tries to re-establish itself. Light pruning, i.e. trimming the tips of plants, encourages the plant to bush out creating a smaller but denser plant. Hard pruning involves the removal of whole branches, which ultimately creates a larger but more open plant. A good general rule to remember is that the harder you prune, the more vigorous the new growth will be.

3. To encourage the plant to produce more flowers or fruit. Cutting off spent flowers before the plant has a chance to produce seed heads should promote more flowers. It is also possible to increase the number of fruiting stems by pruning back older stems. Plants with attractive winter stems, such as dogwood, can be encouraged to produce new, brighter stems if the old stems are cut back.

How to prune

Pruning should always be done with a sharp pair of secateurs, knife or saw depending on the size of branch you need to cut. Never leave a jagged edge and avoid ripping any bark from the tree as this could cause disease. Cut back to a bud or joint, making the cut at an angle so the water will drain away from the bud or down the stem rather than into the bud or joint.

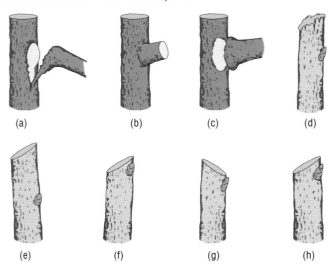

(a)   (b)   (c)   (d)

(e)   (f)   (g)   (h)

incorrect and correct methods of pruning
(a) this shows a branch torn away, leaving a jagged edge that could become diseased
(b) this cut leaves too much stem which may die back and cause disease
(c) here the branch has been cut back too close to the main stem
(d) the cut above the bud has been left ragged
(e) the cut is too high above the bud
(f) the cut is too close to the bud
(g) the cut slopes at the wrong angle
it should face away from the bud to channel rainwater away
(h) this is the correct cut, cleanly sliced, just above the bud and sloping away from it

It is important always to cut back to a bud or joint, even if it means you have to cut off more than you really want to. It is usually best to cut slightly above the bud so you do not risk damaging it, but do not leave too much stem as this will simply die back and could be prone to disease. Choose carefully which bud you cut back to, and check its angle, since the bud will grow to form the new stem. It is usually better to cut to an outward facing bud as this will open up the centre of the plant by encouraging the

the second cut

the first cut

the third cut

when removing a large branch, make an undercut first, then cut away the bulk of the branch
this leaves a manageable length of stem which can be cut off at the correct point just beyond the collar where the branch meets the main stem

branch to grow outwards. Large branches should always be cut in sections to avoid damaging the plant. First make a cut upwards into the branch 15 cm (6 in) or so along from where you want to remove the branch. This will ensure that the branch does not pull away and strip the bark. Then cut the branch off downwards on the outer side of the original cut, i.e. furthest from the trunk or central stem. Once the main branch has been removed you will be left with a manageable length to deal with.

When cutting a branch off from the main stem, be careful not to cut into the collar. This is usually easy to see as the branch widens out where it joins the stem. Again cut at an angle to allow the water to run away harmlessly.

It used to be recommended to paint large cuts with special substances to prevent disease, but on the whole this is now regarded as unnecessary. After pruning, always be sure to feed and water the plant well to help it to recover from the shock.

It is important to be able to distinguish between old and new wood. New growth is usually green and very pliable. Old but living wood is normally brown or grey but will

before

after

after

pruning deciduous spring-flowering shrubs
in summer, after flowering, cut back the stems that have flowered to a strong bud or shoot
if necessary, cut back old stems by a quarter

be green or white underneath the bark. Cuts made back as far as either of these should readily re-grow. Many plants, such as lavender and conifers, develop a woody base that is brown when cut into. Branches cut back as far as this are unlikely to re-grow and will simply die, possibly killing the entire plant.

Generally it is better to cut too little rather than too much. You are extremely unlikely to harm a plant by underpruning it and you can always make more severe cuts next time. Drastic pruning can be used to rejuvenate old or overgrown plants (see p. 70) but it is a kill or cure approach and there is always a considerable element of risk involved.

The main questions with pruning are when to do it and how much to cut off. Most plants should be given three to four years to establish themselves before you start to prune too much. As far as timing is concerned, a very general but useful rule is that you should prune after flowering to allow the plant as much time as possible to

be ready for the next flowering season. With plants that flower later in the summer this pruning is usually delayed until the spring so the new growth is not at risk from frost damage. Apart from one or two exceptions, shrubs can be divided as follows:

Deciduous spring-flowering plants

These mostly flower on stems that have grown over the previous year. Immediately after flowering some of these stems should be removed to allow new shoots to grow up and be ready to flower the following year. The exact timing of the pruning will depend on when the plant finishes flowering. Dead or diseased stems should also be removed. Many of these shrubs do not need much pruning but if you remove some of the old stems it will give the new shoots room to grow and allow the plant to concentrate on developing them. See illustration on p. 65.

Deciduous summer-flowering plants

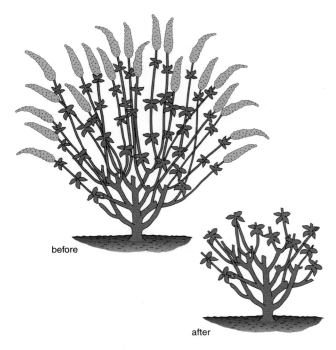

before

after

pruning deciduous summer-flowering shrubs
these should be cut back in early to mid-spring
they flower on new growth and should be cut back more severely than spring-flowering shrubs
cut back all the previous season's growth to within a couple of buds
a permanent woody framework will develop at the base of the plant

These shrubs will flower mostly on this year's growth and should be pruned in the spring to establish plenty of new stems. In effect you are still pruning after flowering, but have waited until the danger of frost is past. It is important not to prune too early as the new growth will be susceptible to frost damage and if this occurs you will have to prune again to remove the damaged tips. These plants usually benefit from harder pruning. Cut back the previous year's growth to a healthy bud, which will then form the new flowering stem. Also cut out any dead or diseased wood and any stems that are growing where you do not want them.

When to prune deciduous-flowering shrubs

Before – Spring: prune early in the season, but after risk of frost is over.
After – Summer: prune after the plant has finished flowering. If the plant flowers early, e.g. winter jasmine, this pruning may actually take place in spring and is indicated below.

Akebia Before
Bignonia Before
Buddleja alternifolia After
B. davidii Before
Campsis Before
Caryopteris Before
Ceanothus Before
Ceratostigma Before
Chaenomeles (Flowering quince) After
Cotoneaster After
Cytisus (Broom) Do not cut into old wood; After
Deutzia After
Forsythia Late spring; After
Fuchsia (hardy) Before
Helianthemum After
Hibiscus syriacus Before
Hydrangea anomola (Climbing Hydrangea) After
Hydrangea Do *not* deadhead in autumn; Before
Jasminium nudiflorum (Winter jasmine) Spring; After
Kerria After
Lavatera (Mallow) Before
Lavendula (Lavender) Do not cut into old wood; Start trimming in first year; After
Lonicera (Honeysuckle) Before
Magnolia After
Parthenocissus Before
Passiflora (Passion flower) After
Philadelphus (Mock orange) After
Plumbago Before

Polygonum Before
Rhododendron and *Azalea* After
Ribes sanguineum (Flowering currant) Late spring; After
Rosmarinus (Rosemary) After
Santolina After
Solanum crispum (Chilean potato plant) Before
Solanum jasminoides Before
Spirea arguta Late spring; After
S. douglasii Before
S. japonica Before
S. prunifolia Late spring; After
S. thunbergii Late spring; After
Syringia (Lilac) After
Tamarix (Tamarisk) Before
Thunbergia Before
Vibernum Late spring; After
Weigela After

Broad-leaved evergreens

These should be pruned in late spring after any risk of frost. All weak, diseased, dead or damaged stems should be removed and any branches you want to shorten should be cut back to a suitably facing bud. Extensive pruning should not be necessary.

Acuba
Camellia
Choisya (Mexican orange)
Elaeagnus
Euonymus
Ilex (Holly)
Lauras noblis (Bay laurel)
Mahonia
Osmanthus

Conifers

These should be pruned in late summer or early autumn. This is because they bleed sap if cut during the growing season, i.e. spring. In this case the risk of damage to new shoots by frost is less serious than sap loss. Dead and diseased wood should be removed but on the whole not much pruning should be necessary. Most conifers will not grow new stems if you cut back into old wood so if you have to make large cuts you may need to retrain other stems to cover the gap. *Taxus* (yew) is the exception and will tolerate harder pruning.

Trees

Most trees should need little pruning except to remove dead or diseased branches. If you have a tree that is in need of major re-shaping, it is usually better to get professional tree surgeons to do the job for you. When cutting large branches, be sure to follow the instructions on p. 65 to minimize any damage to the tree. Crossed branches should be removed to keep the centre of the tree well ventilated but if you keep an eye out you should be able to remove these when they are still small. The timing is roughly the same as for shrubs, i.e. deciduous trees should be pruned after flowering in spring or summer, broad-leaved evergreens in spring and conifers in late summer or early autumn.

Climbers

Apart from the special cases listed below, the basic rules for pruning shrubs can be applied to climbers. Most climbers benefit from yearly pruning to keep them in check rather than a drastic cut back every few years. After pruning ensure any new stems are trained to grow in the direction you want while they are still young and pliable.

Climatis

Pruning clematis is often regarded as a difficult task, but it is in fact perfectly simple as all the plants fall into one of three categories determined by the flowering time. Even if you identify the plant wrongly and cut off too much you are unlikely to do any lasting damage and the plant will probably recover the following year. With all clematis the aims are to control the size and ensure the plant flowers all the way down. If left to themselves most clematis will only flower at the top leaving you with a view of dry, broken stems.

Spring-flowering clematis are:

C. alpina
C. armandii
C. cirrhosa
C. macropetala
C. montana

This group usually has smallish flowers that appear in mid to late spring. You should prune after flowering but only if you want to reduce the size of the plant. If you like, you can cut the plant right back to 30 cm (1 ft) from the base but you must then leave the plant for three years to recover.

Summer-flowering clematis have large flowers that appear in early summer on the previous season's shoots.

They can also flower later in the season on new growth. You should prune in early spring but do not cut off too much as each bud represents a future flower. If the plant gets too big you can either cut it down as for spring-flowering varieties (this will lose the first flush of flowers but the second should do well) or cut one-third of the stems down in spring, one-third down after flowering and the final third the following spring.

C. 'Barbara Jackman'
C. 'Lasurstern'
C. 'Lord Neville'
C. 'Marie Boisselot'
C. 'Mrs N Thompson'
C. 'Nelly Moser'
C. 'Niobe'
C. 'The President'
C. 'Richard Pennell'
C. 'Vyvyan Pennell'

Late summer/early autumn flowering clematis have large flowers in late summer and early autumn on that season's growth. Once the plant is established, it should be pruned every year in late winter or early spring. Cut back to a pair of buds 20–30 cm (8–12 in) above ground. If a branch has no buds, cut it off at ground level and a new stem should re-grow. Obviously the exact height you cut at will depend on the size of plant you want, but the height given above should ensure you have flowers all the way up and down the stems.

C. 'Comtesse de Bouchard'
C. 'Ernest Markham'
C. 'Gipsy Queen'
C. 'Hagley Hibrid'
C. 'Jackmanii'
C. 'Perle d'Azur'
C. tangutica
C. 'Ville de Lyon'
C. viticella

Wisteria

Wisteria looks stunning, but it can be difficult to get it to flower. After planting many will not flower for the first seven years. Once they are established it is important to prune them twice a year to get the maximum number of flowers. In mid-summer, after flowering, all new growth should be cut back to 15 cm (6 in). You can cut the plant back more than once during the summer if it is putting out a lot of new growth. In mid-winter prune again, cutting back all the new growth to two to three buds.

Vines (Vitis)

These should be pruned in early to mid-winter to prevent sap leaking out. Once the framework is established, usually after two to three years, you should shorten all the side shoots to within two to three buds. The main stems will become gnarled and knobbly and look attractive in winter when the plant loses its leaves.

Roses

Unless you are aiming to produce show roses, the pruning of most garden roses is not that complicated. Tests carried out by The Royal National Rose Society showed that large-flowered and cluster-flowered bush roses actually produced a greater quantity of blooms when randomly cut back with electrical hedge cutters. In other words, don't worry too much. As with many other plants, if you do cut off too much you are unlikely to do any lasting damage. Very roughly roses can be divided into four groups: shrub, bush, climbers and ramblers. Pruning rules can be followed for each group. All roses should be deadheaded regularly during the flowering season. At the end of the season you can leave the flowers to form attractive hips on some varieties. To identify roses, refer to Chapter 5.

Shrub roses

These form a wide group including old roses and some repeat-flowering roses. They only need light pruning. After flowering the stems can be reduced by one-third if the plant is getting too large and every three years some old stems can be removed at the base to open up the plant. Any dead or diseased stems should also be removed after flowering.

Bush roses

This type of rose has mostly been developed since the nineteenth century with the aim of producing a succession of flowers. The group also includes Bush Standards, which are bush roses grafted onto a single tall stem. These roses flower repeatedly on the current season's growth and should be pruned in spring so that the new growth is not damaged by frost. On exposed sites the pruning can be carried out in late autumn to prevent any long stems being damaged by winds. Cut away any dead or diseased wood and any stems that are thinner than a pencil. For large-flowered bush roses (hybrid teas) cut stems back to an outward facing bud

20–25 cm (8–10 in) above ground. Cluster-flowered bush roses or floribundas should have their stems shortened to 30–40 cm (12–16 in) above ground. Patio and miniature roses can be pruned in the same way, reducing the stems to prevent congestion.

Climbers

These should be pruned between mid-autumn and early spring. Growth over three years tends to be less productive and should be cut down to a bud, which will then grow into a new, flower-bearing stem. Always ensure about six main stems remain. Prune shoots that have flowered by two-thirds their length back to a bud or shoot.

Ramblers

Prune this group in mid- to late summer after flowering. If you wish to reduce the size, cut a quarter to a third of stems out at the base. If necessary you can also cut the side shoots back but this will not improve flowering as ramblers flower on the same wood for several years.

Hedges

The most important thing with hedges over 1 m (3 ft) high is to cut them at an angle so that leaves grow all the way down.

The top can be flat, curved or pointed, the latter two are better if you get a lot of snow as it tends to sit on a flat-topped hedge and can damage the stems. When planting a hedge, trim it gently and regularly as it grows up, rather

an overgrown hedge can be renovated by cutting one side right back to the main stem
do not trim the other side too much
repeat the process on the other side the following year

than leaving it until it reaches the required height, as this will encourage even growth for the whole height of the hedge.

When trimming hedges by hand always keep the blades parallel to the hedge to ensure the surface is kept flat. Electric trimmers can be useful for long hedges, but do not use them on large-leaved plants as they tend to rip the leaves rather than cutting them neatly. Formally shaped hedges usually need to be trimmed twice a year – winter

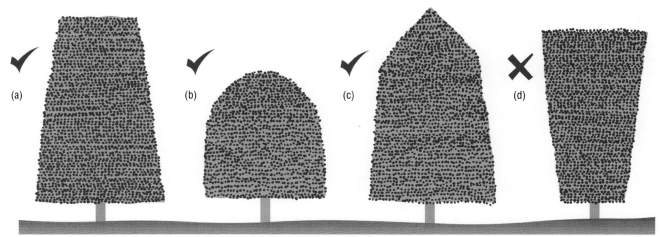

(a) (b) (c) (d)

shapes (a) to (c) are suitable for most types of hedges as light and air can reach all parts
in (d) an area of shadow is created at the base of the plant and stems here will not flourish

and mid-summer for deciduous and late spring and late summer for evergreens. This is particularly important for coniferous hedges as they will not regrow if you cut into old wood. Other types of hedging can be renovated by heavy pruning, which should be carried out in mid-winter for deciduous and mid-spring for evergreen plants. Cut one side of the hedge back to the main stem and trim the other side, then reverse the process the following year, feeding and watering the plants well in between.

If you need to reduce the height of the hedge this must be done at a separate time, either before or after renovating, thus allowing the plants time to recover. Bear in mind this type of pruning can give the plant a great shock that some may not survive.

Drastic pruning

Some overgrown shrubs can be renovated by very hard pruning, but there is always an element of risk involved. If for any reason the plant is irreplaceable, treat it gently and carry out the operation over several seasons.

Plants such as honeysuckle, which develop a lot of brown undergrowth, can be pruned and cleared with garden shears, but be careful not to cut away all the top greenery in the process. If you wish to reduce the entire plant you can cut the main stems back to 30–60 cm (1–2 ft) from the ground.

Deciduous plants should usually be renovated after flowering and evergreens in mid-spring. Cut back one-third to a half of the old stems to about 30 cm (1 ft) and repeat the following year. Plants that can be drastically pruned:

Buddleja davidii should be done in spring
Buxus (Box)
Choisya ternata (Mexican orange plant)
Escallonia
Euonymus fortunei
E. japonicus
Ilex aquifolium (Holly)
Lavatera (Mallow) should be done in spring
Lonicera nitida (Shrub honeysuckle)
L. pileata (Shrub honeysuckle)
Santolina (Lavender cotton)
Taxus (Yew)
Viburnum tinus

Coppicing is a type of hard pruning and is used for plants with attractive winter stems such as *Cornus* (dogwood). It promotes strong new growth, which is usually brightly coloured compared with the older growth. The stems should be cut to a bud 5–8 cm (2–3 in) above ground in early spring.

Deadheading

This is a type of pruning and involves removing dead or faded flowers. The idea behind this is that the plant looks neater and the removal of spent flowers can encourage the growth of more flowers. Obviously you should not deadhead plants such as honesty where the seed heads are an attractive feature. If you want to collect seeds or if you want the plant to self-seed, you should leave the final flush of flowers in place.

The flowerhead should be removed by cutting down to the next bud or joint, removing as little of the stem as possible. Annuals in particular respond to this treatment as they will go on producing flowers until they manage to set seed or the first frosts come. Many perennials such as lupin, geraniums and valerian will also produce more flowers if deadheaded. The most important exception to remember is that you should not deadhead bush *Hydrangeas* – the dead flowerheads act as protection for the plant during winter and should not be removed until you prune in spring.

Propagation

There are a variety of reasons for growing your own plants from seeds or cuttings – it is by far the cheapest way to stock your garden, it is an extremely rewarding and fairly simple activity and you can have exactly what you want, not what the garden centre dictates.

There are four main methods of propagation: seed sowing, taking cuttings, division and layering. If you get hooked on propagating your own plants, further reading is listed in the bibliography at the back of the book.

Seed sowing is a good way of raising many annuals, biennials, vegetables and some perennials. It can also be used for trees and shrubs, but taking cuttings is usually a better and quicker method for these plants. How to raise plants from seed is described below.

Cuttings involve taking part of a plant and encouraging it to grow its own roots and become a separate plant. They can be taken from trees, shrubs and perennials and are particularly useful if you want to reproduce a plant exactly. With seeds, variations may occur, particularly if the plant has been specially bred.

Division is mostly used for multiplying your perennials. Basically, the plant is dug up and divided into smaller parts, which are then replanted to form new plants.

Layering is a good technique for clematis and shrubs with branches that grow close to the ground. Some plants, such as ivy, will layer themselves. The technique of layering involves burying part of a branch attached to the main plant under the soil to encourage it to grow roots. Once the new roots have established themselves, the branch can be cut off from the main plant and thus a new plant is formed.

Seeds

It is remarkably easy to grow plants from seeds. All that seeds need to germinate and grow are soil, water, warmth and light. In a short growing time seeds will turn into a large number of plants and it is both fascinating and satisfying to watch them growing day by day.

Seeds fall into three main groups:

Half-hardies

These are annuals or perennials that are unable to survive the frost. They should be sown in late winter or early spring in a sheltered environment (this could be in a cold frame or a part of the garden that is not exposed) and planted out in summer when there is no danger of frost. Examples of these are alyssum, Busy Lizzies or impatience (*Impatiens*), lavatera, lobelia, tobacco plants (*Nicotiana*), *Pentunias*, Sunflowers (*Helianthus*) and snapdragons (*Antirrhinums*).

Hardy annuals

These plants are capable of withstanding frost and can be sown in mid spring out of doors. Opium poppies (*Papaver somniferum*), cornflowers (*Centaurea cyanus*) and sweet peas (*Lathrus odoratus*) are examples of this type of plant.

Perennials and biennials

These are usually sown in early to mid-summer out of doors so that they can establish roots and leaves ready to flower the following summer. Examples of these are foxgloves (*Digitalis*), hollyhocks (*Alcea*), sweet williams (*Dianthus barbatus*) and wallflowers (*Erysimum cheiri* syn *Cheiranthus*). Many herbs and vegetables can also be successfully grown from seed. Examples are given in the relevant sections: vegetables, p. 100; herbs, p. 110.

Although it is very satisfying to collect and grow your own seeds, to begin with it is worth buying packets of seeds as they will come with valuable advice for growing that particular plant. The information that follows is generally applicable to most seeds, but planting depths and light requirements can vary considerably. The seed packet will also give you advice on sowing and planting times.

Equipment

Most seeds respond better to being grown in trays as they can be given good soil and moved to a suitable environment once they are big enough. Plastic trays are the easiest to use and are usually 35 × 20 cm (14 × 8 in). Half and quarter sizes are also available. Most garden centres stock them and they are cheap and can be reused as long as you wash them well with detergent. Be careful to avoid the really cheap flimsy ones as they will be harder to move and you will run the risk of upsetting them and losing all your plants. Plug trays – plant trays that have been divided so each seedling has its own hole – are also available. This allows the plants to develop good root systems without the danger of them mixing with adjacent plants. They are midway between a tray and an individual pot and are particularly suitable for plants such as basil, which dislike root disturbance. Depending on the type you are using, when the time comes to plant on the seedling you either push the soil and root ball out from the base or separate the two sides of the plug. Individual flowerpots are also useful for larger plants. Try to buy square ones as they are much more effective in terms of space. Originally all flowerpots were made of clay and it was easier to make them round in shape, but with plastic this is no longer the case. Your seedlings may look more attractive in terracotta pots, but square plastic ones are much more practical.

You will need a sterile compost in which to grow the seeds. Young seedlings are very susceptible to disease and stand a better chance of surviving if they are grown in a pure medium. All ready-mixed composts are sterile and these have the added advantage that you can choose the soil to match the plant. Many seeds need a specialized seed compost to start them off, but if you have to use this you will need to transplant the seedlings as they get bigger as it does not contain enough nutrients to support a growing plant. Never be tempted to use the soil from the garden, however well your plants seem to grow in it, and do not reuse compost as the previous batch of seedlings will have used up all the goodness. Vermiculite or perlite is available at garden centres and is a volcanic mineral that can be put on the top of the soil to stop it drying out or mixed into it to make it easier for the new roots to grow. It is very light and easily allows the roots to grow through it.

A watering can with a fine rose on it will allow you to water the seedlings gently and a mist sprayer will enable you to water them when they are too delicate even for a fine spray. Mist sprayers are cheap and easily available and you will need a watering can almost regardless of the size of your garden.

A clear covering for the seed trays will be necessary while the seedlings germinate. You can either use clingfilm or sheets of Perspex or glass. Clear plastic freezer bags will also create the correct environment for germination, i.e. warmth and damp.

Unless you are only growing one type of seed, you will need labels and a pencil or waterproof pen. You should get into the habit of always marking a tray with the plant and date the minute you plant it as trays of seeds look identical and even seedlings can be extremely hard to identify.

A dibber or lolly stick is useful for planting seeds and, lastly, you will need a widger – a small wooden spoon-like tool – for lifting seedlings. An old spoon or wide lolly stick can often be used instead.

If you get keen on growing plants from seed, it may be worth investing in a propagator. These vary enormously in size and complexity, but are basically portable containers which, to a greater or lesser extent, mimic the conditions in a greenhouse. They have space for trays of seeds, clear tops to allow light in and some have underfloor thermostatic heating. Most seeds need a temperature between 15–20 °C (59–68 °F) to germinate

and even if you have a greenhouse you will probably not want the entire building at this temperature. Propagators allow you to create a microclimate but are not necessary for all seeds. Many will quite happily germinate if placed in a light, warm position such as a windowsill. The best way to choose a propagator is to go to a large, reputable garden centre and ask advice once you have first worked out your requirements. The main advantages of propagators are that they allow you to start sowing seeds earlier in the year (thereby conning nature into giving you more crops, flowers, etc.), they speed up germination and greatly increase the success rate with trickier plants.

Look at the charts on p. 75 to see which method is most suitable for the plants you have chosen. Some can be planted directly in the soil where they are to grow, whereas others need to be grown in trays or pots and then planted out.

Indoor tray method

Fill the seed tray or pots to about a centimetre (half an inch) below the rim with compost and gently press down till the surface is level. Some seeds need to be planted in special seed compost, otherwise use general purpose mixtures. Then water the compost thoroughly and leave to drain. It is better to water the base soil before you put the seeds in, otherwise they might be washed too far down in the soil.

The growers' instructions on the seed packet will tell you how far apart to plant the seeds. It is a very common mistake to plant the seeds too thickly – they will not grow so well and you will have the task of thinning out the little seedlings. It is usually easier to pour the seeds into your hand and then spread them on the soil rather than trying to sprinkle them directly from the packet. If the seeds are very small, it is easiest to mix them with sand before trying to scatter them. Not all the seeds will germinate, but try to spread them out so that each seed has room to grow. There is no point producing more plants than you can use and many seeds can be stored for use next year. As a rough guide, allow enough space for a seedling with two or three pairs of leaves to grow up.

Cover the seeds with a layer of compost, ideally using a fine sieve, but if you do not have one try to crumble the soil so it is as fine as possible. The depth needed will vary. Larger seeds usually need to be planted at a greater depth 1.5–3 cm (½–1 in) whereas very fine seeds need not be covered at all. A layer of vermiculite or perlite can then be placed over the soil. This looks like polystyrene, but is actually a type of volcanic rock. It is very useful as it prevents the soil from drying out but is also very light and allows the seedlings to grow through it easily.

Finally moisten the soil with a mist sprayer and label the tray. Cover with a clear layer that will keep the moisture in but allow light to penetrate. Clingfilm or large clear freezer bags firmly secured are probably the easiest option, but sheets of glass or Perspex can also be used. Some seeds need to be kept in the dark in order to germinate (see chart on p. 75) so cover the top with black plastic or several layers of newspaper.

Seeds can take from two to 28 days to germinate, but as soon as the shoots start appearing remove the covering and ensure the tray receives plenty of light and air and remains moist but not wet. More seedlings die from overwatering than anything else. The seed trays should not be placed in direct sunlight as seedlings are very delicate and will easily shrivel up if overheated.

Pricking out is the next stage and involves thinning the seedlings to eliminate the weaker plants and give the stronger ones room to grow. You can either do this by pulling up the weaker plants or by transplanting the stronger ones. This usually needs to be done two to three weeks after germination when the seedlings have a couple of pairs of proper leaves, not just the cotyledons or seed leaves that appear first. The easiest method is simply to remove the unwanted plants, either by hand or using a pair of tweezers. Water the tray a couple of hours beforehand so the seedlings will come up easily. If necessary push the soil back down around the remaining plants using your fingers or a widger (flat plant labels or wide lolly sticks are also fine).

If you grew the seeds in a tray using seed compost, you will now need to transplant the seedlings to give them sufficient nutrients to continue growing strongly. Water the seedlings and fill the new trays or pots with a suitable sterile compost mixture up to about one centimetre (half an inch) from the top. For most plants a general purpose mixture is fine. Water and leave to drain. Make holes in the new compost about 5 cm (2 in) apart using a dibber, blunt pencil, lolly stick or your finger. With the widger, gently lift a clump of seedlings from the tray. Separate the plants by holding the leaves (the stems and roots are very fragile and should not be touched) and gently lower each

one into a hole. Push the soil back round the plant ensuring all the roots are covered. When you have finished, water the newly planted seedlings very gently. Do not worry if the plants droop at first. They have had a huge shock but should recover quite easily.

As the plants grow bigger, it may be necessary to repeat the procedure again before they can be planted out in the garden. As a general rule, if in doubt give plants too much room rather than too little. Overcrowded plants do not do well and most need gaps of 5–8 cm (2–3 in).

Plants that are grown indoors or in a sheltered environment need to be hardened off before they can be planted out in the garden. On mild days, put the plants outside in a sheltered position starting with a couple of hours and building this up over a two-week period. This will allow the plants to become acclimatized gradually to outdoor life. For planting out follow the instructions on p. 55.

Sowing directly outdoors method

This method is much easier as the seeds are sown directly into the patch of ground where you want them to grow, but it is only applicable for certain plants (see the chart on p. 75). Timing is particularly important for outdoor sowing as there is no point putting seeds into soil where they will be unable to germinate. Traditionally farmers dropped their trousers and sat on the earth to test whether it was warm enough to sow, but it is just as easy to tell by feeling the soil with your hands! If it feels cold and clammy, wait a few days. If you keep a gardening diary, remember that the soil will not necessarily warm up at the same time each year.

When the soil is ready, fork it over and finely rake it, being careful not to disrupt any existing plants and bulbs. If you wish to plant the seeds in straight rows, mark them using pegs and string (see the diagram on p. 74).

Even if you wish the plants to appear randomly, it is worth planting them in a regular pattern so that you can easily distinguish between the seedlings and any weeds that grow up. Diagonal crosses with a stick at each corner are easy to monitor and will disappear when the plants grow up.

Make a shallow furrow using a dibber, stick or the edge of the rake. Be careful not to bury the seeds too deeply

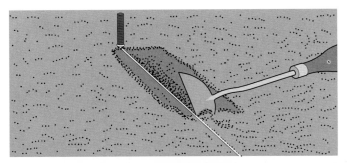

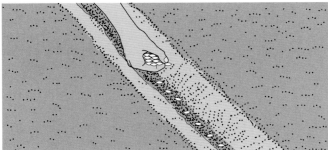

how to sow seeds in a straight line using pegs and string

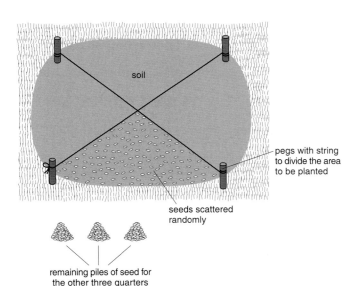

soil

pegs with string
to divide the area
to be planted

seeds scattered
randomly

remaining piles of seed for
the other three quarters

by dividing the area to be sown using pegs and string, you can scatter the seeds randomly
it is easier to create a balanced effect over a large area if you divide both seeds and land into manageable portions

otherwise they will fail to germinate. Spread the seeds evenly along the row allowing enough room for the grown plant and then cover with soil using the rake. Make sure you label the seeds clearly and firmly embed the label in the soil.

If you wish the plants to grow completely randomly, scatter them over the area and then rake the soil over them. If using this method you will have to be very careful to make sure that weeds do not grow up and smother the young plants.

As the plants grow they can be thinned if necessary using the same method as for indoor seedlings. The excess plants can be planted elsewhere or discarded. Ideally try not to overcrowd the plants in the first place as some plants grown using this method do not like to be moved. Remember to keep the young plants well watered and feed with a liquid food.

Outdoor seedbed method

This is a useful method, which is like a cross between sowing seeds directly into the ground and germinating them in a seed tray. The advantage of it is that the seeds can germinate in an inconspicuous area outside and be transplanted to their flowering position once they have grown to a suitable height. The soil must be well prepared (see section on digging on p. 48) and the site sheltered and sunny. Plant the seeds following the instructions for directly sown seeds. It is often advisable to cover the area with about a centimetre (half an inch) of sharp sand. In effect this acts as a protective layer; it prevents the soil from drying out and forming a hard crust, it enables water to penetrate and easily allows the seedlings to grow up through it. If necessary thin the seedlings when they have two to three pairs of leaves, water well, feed unless your soil is very fertile and plant on at the appropriate time.

Self-seeding

Many garden plants will self-seed naturally as they would in the wild. Simply leave the seedheads on the plants and allow nature to do the work for you. Obviously the position and growth of the seedlings will be haphazard, but you can easily move the young plants if they are trying to grow where you do not want them. Seeds from neighbouring gardens may also appear in your garden as a result of matter carried in the wind or by birds and animals.

A selection of plants which can easily be grown from seed

Plant and type	How to sow	When to sow	Notes
Alcea (Hollyhock) P	In pots out-of-doors under glass.	Mid–late winter.	Perennials but better grown as annual or biennial. Can sow direct in early summer to flower the following summer.
Ageratum HHA	Surface sow. Indoor tray. Light cover with vermiculite.	Early spring.	Plant out in late spring after last frost. Needs good light to germinate.
Antirrhinum (Snapdragon) HHA	Indoor tray. Surface sow.	Late winter/ early spring.	In mild areas for earlier flowers sow seeds in mid summer and plant in situ in early autumn.
Campanula medium (Canterbury bells) B	Seed bed.	Late spring/ early summer.	Plant in flowering position in autumn.
Centaurea (Cornflower) P	Direct.	Mid-spring.	Can be sown in early autumn in mild areas.
Dianthus barbaratus (Sweet william) B	Seedbed.	Late spring.	Plant up mid-autumn to flower following year.
Dianthus chinensis Pinks HA	Indoor tray.	Early spring.	Sow direct in mid spring in mild areas.
Digitalis (Foxglove) B	Seedbed.	Late spring/ early summer.	Plant up in autumn.
Erisimum cheiri syn *Cheiranthus* (Wallflower) B	Seedbed.	Late spring/ early summer.	Plant out in mid-autumn. For bushy plant pinch out tips when 15 cm (6 in) tall.
Eschscholzia Californian poppy HA	Direct.	Early–mid-spring or early autumn.	Dislikes being moved. Should self-seed easily.
Gazania HHA	Indoor tray.	Early autumn.	Plant out in late spring after frosts.
Helianthus annus (Sunflower) HA	Direct 2.5 cm (1 in) deep.	Mid-spring.	
Lathyrus odoratus (Sweet pea) HA	Pots.	Mid-autumn.	Overwinter in cold frame. Plant out early–mid-spring. Alternatively sow direct early–mid-spring.
Lavatera trimestris (Mallow) HA	Direct.	Early spring.	Can be sown early autumn in mild areas.
Limnanthes douglasii HA	Direct.	Early spring.	In mild areas can be sown direct in early autumn to give earlier flowers.
Lobularia maritima (Sweet alyssum) HA	Indoor tray.	Late winter.	Plant out in late spring. Alternatively seeds can be sown directly out of doors in mid spring.
Lunaria (Honesty) B	Seedbed.	Late spring/ early summer.	Plant in situ in early autumn or early spring.
Mesembryanthemum HHA	Indoor tray under compost.	Late winter/ early spring.	Needs dark to germinate.
Myosotis (Forget-me-not) B	Seedbed.	Mid–late spring.	Plant up in early to mid-autumn. Alternatively can sow directly in situ in spring.
Nemesia HHA	Indoor tray.	Early spring.	Alternatively sow seeds direct in mid-spring
Nicotiana (Tobacco plant) HHA	Indoor tray.	Late winter/ early spring.	Plant out after last frost in late spring.

continued

A selection of plants which can easily be grown from seed – *continued*

Plant and type	How to sow	When to sow	Notes
Nigella (Love-in-a-mist) HA	Direct.	Early spring.	Can sow in autumn in mild climate.
Papaver nudicaule (Icelandic poppy) P	Direct.	Autumn. Spring.	For flowering late spring/early summer, For flowering mid–late summer.
Papaver somniferum (Opium poppy) HA	Direct.	Mid-spring.	Can sow early autumn in mild areas.
Petunia HHA	Indoor tray.	Early spring.	Very fine seeds. Mix with sand and surface sow.
Phlox HHA	Indoor tray.	Early spring.	Sow direct in mid-spring in mild areas.
Tagetes (African and French marigolds) HHA	Indoor tray. Lightly cover with compost.	Early–mid spring.	Plant out in late spring after late frost.
Tropaeolum (Nasturtium) HA	Indoor tray.	Late winter.	Alternatively sow seeds direct in mid-spring.
Verbena HHA	Indoor tray. Surface sow. Cover with vermiculite.	Early spring.	Plant out after last frost in late spring.
Viola (Pansy) P/HA/B	Seedbed 0.5–1 cm (¼–½ in) deep. Seedbed 0.5–1 cm (¼–½ in) deep.	Early–late summer. Early–mid autumn.	For autumn flowering. For spring flowering.
Zinnia HHA	Indoor tray.	Early spring.	Plant out after last frost in late spring.

HHA – Half hardy annual, HA – Hardy annual, B – Biennial, P – Perennial

Possible problems

If your seeds fail to germinate, the chances are that you have provided the wrong sort of conditions. Seeds you collect yourself are always unpredictable but most seeds bought in a packet should germinate if you follow the instructions. Check you planted them at the correct depth, gave them the correct levels of light and heat and neither too much water nor too little.

Once the seedlings have grown, their greatest danger is from a disease called 'damping off'. This causes the seedlings to wilt, collapse and eventually die. To prevent this, ensure that all containers are thoroughly washed with detergent and well rinsed before using them. Clean your tools, only use a fresh, sterile growing medium and water from the tap rather than water stored in a barrel, which may contain germs that the young plant is not strong enough to fight. Finally, ensure there is enough space between each plant for the air to circulate.

Lawns

The picture that springs to mind when most people think of a garden is that of a lawn surrounded by flowerbeds. This is undoubtedly one of the most common arrangements for a garden but it is by no means the only option. If you decide that you do want a lawn, it is worth considering what sort of grass you want and what sort of treatment it is going to receive, in terms of wear and tear and mowing.

In many small gardens it is not really worth having a lawn. Grass does not grow well if it is in the shade for much of the day, which is often the case in a small space. Also, if you have a small garden you are liable to put too much strain on the grass and it will not thrive. That said, if you really want grass – and there is much in its favour, not least lying out on it on a hot sunny day – be prepared to look after it well and possibly to replace it every five or ten years.

a finely cut lawn with stripes

There are many different types of lawns, ranging from fine striped sward through rough playing field to a meadow. If laying a lawn from scratch, it is worth making sure you get the right type of grass for your requirements. Fine lawns are made up of bents and fescues. Fescue is a good general lawn grass while bents are very fine grass and need to be kept short. This is the mixture to go for if you want a beautiful lawn with stripes, but remember it will need a lot of maintenance to look good. Utility grass will contain a higher percentage of meadow grass and rye grasses, which are coarser-leaved and generally tougher. Lawns are the cheapest and usually the easiest way of covering large areas of ground and for this purpose it is important that you choose the appropriate mixture.

Lawn requirements

1. Ideally lawns need a light loam soil that drains well and is not compacted or waterlogged. Light sandy soils should have compost added and heavy clay soils should have sand dug in to improve drainage.

2. Reasonable levels of sunshine are also important – this is why lawns rarely do well in small enclosed gardens.

3. A lawn will not survive being tramped over regularly. If there is a route you frequently take across your lawn, it is usually worth constructing a path or inserting stepping stones in the grass. This is especially necessary in winter when the grass may be damp or frozen and therefore more vulnerable. For the same

reason you should not grass right up to the house or on heavily used walkways, such as from the house to the garage, garden gate or patio.

Seeds versus turf

If you are starting a lawn from scratch, not only do you have to choose the correct type of grass, but also to decide whether to use seed or turf. Turf can be laid at any time as long as the weather is not too hot, too dry or too frosty. Turf will give you an instant effect and can be walked on quicker than grass grown from seeds, but works out about ten times more expensive. In terms of preparation there is not much to choose between the two, although turves are heavy to move when you get round to the actual laying and must be in place within a couple of days of being delivered. Seed is easier to use for unusually shaped areas. After sowing, the area must be protected from birds, who will eat the seeds, and cats who will regard the area as a giant litter tray! Both can be deterred by erecting small stakes round the area and running black cotton thread around and across it. The other risk to new seedlings is weeds that will establish themselves, smother the new grass and use up the nutrients in the soil. As a rough guideline, turf is usually best for a small area or where you need an instant effect and seeds are better if you want to grass a large area cheaply. In the long run seeds may also produce a better lawn as you will be able to choose the exact seed mix you use.

Preparation

If you are starting from scratch you should prepare the soil well. Clear away all weeds, stones and other debris and then dig in compost, and sharp sand if the drainage is poor. If it is very bad you may need to install drainage pipes, but this is one of those jobs best done by professionals. Level the site using a rake, and spade if necessary. Gentle undulations are fine, but small bumps and hollows will make mowing much harder. Having levelled the site, ideally you should leave it for a month so you can pull up any weeds that germinate. Choosing a fine day when the soil is not too damp, you then need to flatten it by 'treading'. This involves walking across the site with your feet close together and taking tiny steps with the pressure on your heels (obviously wearing flat shoes or boots). Once the whole site is flattened, rake it again and then apply a granular fertilizer according to the manufacturer's instructions. If you want a really flat surface, use a spirit level on a plank of wood. It is important that your lawn has a neat edge – corrugated metal or plastic strips can be buried around the grass or you can put down brick or paved edging. Any hard edging must be laid below the level of the grass to allow mowing.

Sowing

Choose the correct seed mixture according to your needs and scatter over the site following the instructions. It is important that you follow the quantities accurately. If you sow the grass too thinly weeds will grow up in between and if you sow it too thickly the individual plants will not thrive. If possible you should sow in mid spring or early autumn when the weather is warm to encourage germination. Straight edges can be marked out with posts and string and curves with a hose. Put plastic sheeting along the edge of the proposed lawn and sprinkle the seed so it goes over the plastic – this will ensure the grass grows thickly right up to the edge of the lawn. To ensure that you scatter the seed evenly, work out how much seed you need in total and, depending on the size of your plot, divide the area and seed into four or six portions. This will give you a smaller area to scatter seed over and you are less likely to scatter it too thinly or thickly. When you have finished, gently rake over the area to spread a fine covering of soil over the seeds. Then water gently and put up canes and twine to deter birds and cats. The seeds will take about three weeks to grow and should be ready for use after about ten weeks. Do not cut until at least 5 cm (2 in) long and water regularly throughout the first growing season.

Turf

Be careful when choosing turf. Cheap turves may contain a high percentage of weeds! Also avoid meadow turf unless you actually want to create a meadow. The soil should be prepared in the same way as for sowing and ideally the turves should be laid within 48 hours of their arrival. If this is not possible, then lay them on plastic or paving, grass side up, in a shady spot and keep well watered. Turf can be laid at any time of year but the soil should be moist rather than wet or dry. When laying turves, stagger the rows and push the edges up close together as the turf may shrink slightly.

If you need to add a piece to complete a row, do it in the middle rather than at an end as it will be less likely to dry out. Once you have laid all the turves, use the back of a rake or a light roller to flatten them and get rid of any air pockets. If you need to cut curves, lay the whole turf and then mark the curve by trailing sand from a funnel along the exact line. You can then trim the turves using a spade or half-moon cutter.

Turf usually establishes itself more quickly than seeded grass and can be used after about four to six weeks.

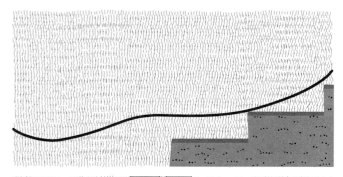

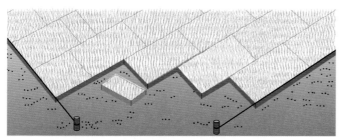

lay turf with the joins staggered and small pieces inserted in the middles of rows rather than at the edges where they are prone to drying out

to create a curved edge to the lawn, mark the exact shape using a funnel and sand or the hose

cut along the line using a spade or half-moon cutter

During this time and after, water well. Turves need more water than seeds as the water has to penetrate right down to the roots.

Maintenance

The type of lawn you have will govern how much care it needs, but all grass requires a certain amount of maintenance.

Mowing

Grass should be cut regularly, partly to keep it looking neat, but also to prevent weeds and moss establishing themselves. When the grass is growing mid-spring to mid-autumn you will need to cut it about once a week, but if the weather gets very hot either leave it or cut it less frequently to prevent the grass from being scorched and turning brown. Similarly, from mid-autumn onwards do not cut the grass too short (2.5 cm/1 in or slightly longer is probably the best length to leave it) as the longer length will protect it from frost during the winter. You should also avoid walking on frosty grass as you can damage it. Utility lawn should be cut to about 2.5 cm (1 in) and fine lawn to 1 cm (½ in) during the mowing season. If your grass gets very long, do not cut it back in one go – it is much less of a shock for the grass if you reduce its height gradually over two to three mowings. The same goes for the first cut of spring, which should only remove the top 1 cm (½ in) of grass. For information on mowers see Chapter 4.

Watering

Lawns should be watered regularly especially during hot weather. With new lawns in particular, it is better to water little and often rather than soaking them as much of the water will sink through the soil and be lost.

Top dressing and feeding

Most utility lawns will never need feeding. However, fine lawns will require some sort of food as continuous cutting removes nutrients from the blades of grass. If you cut little and often you can leave the cuttings to sink back into the soil, but do not let them form a soggy mat as this will do more harm than good. Lawns can be fed in spring and autumn – a variety of feeds are available, some of which also contain weedkiller. Be careful to select the right one for your requirements and always follow the instructions. The spring feed should be nitrogen based to encourage new growth and the autumn feed should be a more balanced general feed.

Top dressing is a useful mixture for applying to any gaps, like in between turves. You can buy it ready mixed or make your own using three parts soil, six parts sand and one part organic compost.

Edging

A neatly edged lawn will automatically look better, even if you do not cut the grass itself. The choice of equipment available to do the edging is covered in Chapter 4. Lawns can be reshaped once or twice a year, if necessary, using a half-moon cutter, but remember you are cutting away lawn that will not grow back.

Aerating

If your lawn is used a lot the soil beneath it can become compacted and will not drain properly. Ideally you should aerate your lawn every three years, but this is probably over-optimistic for most people. Aerating should be carried out in the autumn, after the grass has been cut and when it is neither too wet nor too dry. Use a garden fork or specially designed aerator, which has hollow tines, and push your tool 5 cm (2½ in) into the soil. Ease it back and forth, remove and repeat at 15-cm (6-in) intervals. The hollow-tined aerator removes small plugs of earth, which can be cleared away by brushing later. Aerating is hard work, particularly if your soil is heavy, and for large areas it is probably better to hire a powered machine. The holes will improve drainage, allow fertilizer to penetrate to the roots and make moss less likely to grow. Spread top dressing over the lawn (3 kg per sq m/6 lb per sq yd) and brush into the holes. Do not worry if some of the dressing remains visible. It will soon sink down.

Scarifying

With time thatch can develop at the base of the grass stems. This is a mixture of dead and living organic matter and if it gets too thick it can prevent water, air and fertilizer penetrating the soil. As the problem gets worse the grass will become weaker and more prone to disease. To remove thatch choose an autumn day when the soil is moist and rake the lawn over using a spring-tined rake (see Chapter 4). Apply a top dressing afterwards and be warned that the lawn will actually look much worse when you have finished! The benefits will not be apparent until the new growth comes up in the spring.

Sweeping

You should always sweep any fallen leaves from your

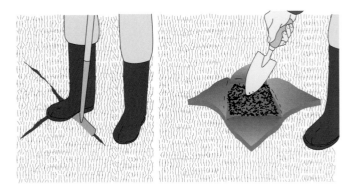

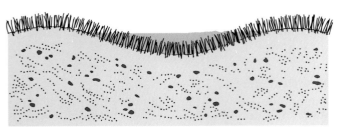

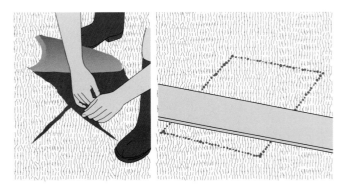

small dips can be infilled using a mixture of top dressing and sand

adjust the amount of sand to suit your soil, i.e. add less if the soil is a heavy clay and more if very light and sandy

to level bumps or hollows in the lawn, cut a cross and peel the turf back

remove or add soil as necessary and then replace the flaps of turf ensuring the surface is level by using a plank of wood as shown

lawn as they will quickly become a soggy mat and prevent air and light reaching the grass.

Problems

If you maintain your lawn well it should have comparatively few problems.

Levelling

Your lawn may develop bumps or hollows as the result of either soil compaction or simply being used. The easiest way to repair this is to cut a cross over the area with a spade and fold the flaps of turf back.

You can then add or remove soil as necessary. To repair minor dips you can simply fill them in with sand, which will gradually work its way into the soil and level out the dip. Both treatments are best carried out in spring when the grass will quickly recover.

Weeds

According to your viewpoint, daisies and buttercups may be charming additions to your lawn or highly invasive weeds. If you wish to use it, weedkiller can be highly effective and should be applied in spring or summer following the manufacturer's instructions. Some products also include fertilizer, but if the one you use does not you should feed the lawn after treating with weedkiller to encourage the grass to grow and fill the gaps. The other alternative is to dig each weed out by hand as it appears. A good method, particularly for dandelions which have deep roots, is to dig vertically down round the plant with an old kitchen knife. Lever the knife so you can remove the plug of earth surrounding the weed – being careful to remove all the root otherwise it will simply re-grow.

Moss

The presence of moss means your lawn is not in good condition. Lack of aeration, too much or too little water, too much shade or lack of nutrients in the soil can all be

grass and wild flower seeds have been sown together here to create a meadow

causes. The most reliable way to get rid of moss is to use a moss killer, take the dead moss away (if you rake up living moss it can spread even more) and then set about trying to remedy the initial cause. If the moss is very persistent, it might be worth making a feature of it and planting perennials in between.

Shade

Specially formulated seed mixes are available for shady areas, but if the area is very dark you might be better to consider using ground-cover plants (see below).

Altering an existing lawn

Boring expanses of lawns can easily be made more interesting so think twice before you dig it all up.

Reshaping

Giving a lawn curved edges can greatly increase the interest and sense of movement. You may not even need to buy more grass as you can move turf from one area to another. Mark the area of turf to be lifted and cut it with a spade into turf-sized pieces (30–45 cm/12–18 in). The trick is to have the pieces as large as you can manage without them breaking as there will then be fewer joins. Slide the spade under the turf 2.5 cm (1 in) below the surface. You should re-lay the turf as soon as possible and water well until it is established. Remember that curved lawns may look more interesting but are harder to mow, so do not make the curves too intricate.

Paths

Paths or stepping stones across a lawn can break it up and make it look more interesting. Surprisingly, curving paths can make a long narrow lawn actually look wider but do not make the path too wiggly as people will tend to ignore it and simply walk up the grass. Also make sure the path leads somewhere. If it simply goes to the end of the garden you could add interest by placing a seat or statue there. Ensure the level of the path or stones is below the grass so it will be easy to mow.

Island bed

A large lawn can be broken up by an island bed, but make sure the bed is large enough to look like a feature in its own right. Statues and trees can also be used to create interest, but bear in mind that any grass beneath a tree is liable to suffer. Suitable trees for lawns include:

Acer (Maple)
Malus (Crab apple)
Prunus (Flowering almond and cherry)
Quercus robus (English oak)
Sorbus (Mountain ash or whitebeam)

Bulbs

Bulbs can be planted within the lawn to give interest in spring. For a natural look you should scatter the bulbs and plant them where they fall, bearing in mind that most look better in drifts or clumps rather than planted singly. You will need to leave the grass uncut around them for six weeks and for this reason they are often better planted at the sides or end of the lawn. Using a bulb planter, as described on p. 55, is the easiest way to plant a lot of bulbs as it makes an exact hole and you can replace the plug of soil and turf back over the bulb. For the best results bulbs should be fed each autumn.

Good bulbs to plant in lawns are:

Chionodoxa (Glory-of-the-snow)
Crocus
Galanthus (Snowdrop)
Narcissus (Daffodil)

Ground cover plants

Depending on the situation and use of the area there are a number of plants that can be used to create non-grass lawns or areas of slightly taller ground cover. Non-grass lawns will usually only cope with a certain amount of traffic and may still need hand weeding and for these reasons they are usually best suited to small areas.

Chamaemelum nobile (Chamomile)
This needs full sun and well-drained soil. It will need to be weeded for the first few years until it is established, but thereafter it will only need trimming.

Menta requienii (Creeping Corsican mint)
This is suitable for damp, shady areas. It provides good cover, has attractive purple flowers and can be walked on a little but dies back in winter.

Moss
In areas of dense damp shade, a moss lawn can be attractive.

Thymus (Thyme)
There are many varieties of creeping thyme, which require similar conditions to chamomile. Be careful when walking on or near them as they attract bees.

Ground cover plants do exactly what they say and cover the ground thereby preventing weeds and filling an area that might otherwise be hard to plant, e.g. shade. Be careful, though, as many ground cover plants tend to be invasive and can take over the garden and become weeds themselves.

Ground cover for sun
Aubretia
Ceanothus (Prostrate ceanothus)
Erica (Heather)
Geranium (Cranesbill)
Helianthemum (Rock rose)
Juniperus (Prostrate juniper)
Lysimachia
Nepeta (Catmint)
Nummularia (Creeping Jenny)
Rosmarinus officinalis (Prostrate varieties of rosemary)
Salvia officinalis (Sage)
Santolina (Lavender cotton)
Sedum spectabile
Stachys byzantina (Lamb's ears)

Ground cover for shade
Ajuga reptans (Bugle)
Bergenia Best in dry shade
Brunnera macrophylla Best in dry shade
Euphorbia robbiae (Spurge) Best in dry shade
Geranium macrorrhizum (Cranesbill) Best in dry shade
Hosta Best in moist shade
Lamium maculatum (Dead nettle) Best in dry shade
Pulmonaria
Saxifraga x urbium (London pride)
Waldsteina

Ground cover for any position
Alchemilla mollis (Lady's mantle)
Cotoneaster (Prostrate)
Hedera (Ivy)
Hypericum calcyinum
Polygonum
Stachys olympia
Vinca major and *minor* (Periwinkle)

containers

Regardless of the size or aspect of your garden, by using containers you will be able to grow a huge variety of plants, from a tree to an array of fruit and vegetables and right down to the tiniest alpine. The only thing you need to remember is that you are not growing the plants in their natural environment and that they will therefore need a little more attention than those growing directly in the soil. The advantage is that you have almost complete control of the growing conditions. You can create a micro-environment within the container, which will give you a much greater choice of the plants you can grow. This means you can grow plants that would not normally survive in the soil in your garden, such as camellias, which need an acid soil. Since plants grown in containers can be moved, you can also grow plants that might not survive all year round in a regular flowerbed – tender plants can be taken inside during winter or moved to a more protected spot in the garden.

Containers are invaluable for providing interest in an otherwise drab area of the garden. They are particularly useful if you are waiting for something to grow up – you can either place them at the edge of the flowerbed or hide them amongst existing plants within the bed. Some plants, such as lilies, are ideal for this purpose since they will flourish in containers even when their roots are constricted. If you do place pots within the bed, be careful that you do not position them so that they shade or impede the growth of nearby plants. Another advantage of containers is that you can move them around the garden to give seasonal interest, for example to provide colour after early perennials have finished flowering.

Almost any plant can be grown in a container as long as the roots have enough room to grow and you provide them with adequate food and water. Many trees and shrubs will not reach their full size as their roots will always be constricted however large the pot is, but this does not necessarily do the plant any harm. If you keep them trimmed, the plants will not grow leggy and this method allows you to grow trees and large shrubs in situations where they would otherwise over-run the garden.

Containers can also be used to disguise an unsightly part of the garden. Tall or climbing plants grown in a row of containers will effectively cover an unattractive but useful shed. You can position containers to soften features such as doors and fences or emphasize a change in the garden, such as the edge of a patio or a flight of steps.

Large containers can be ornaments in their own right and some do not even need to be planted up. As a general rule ornate pots look better with a simple planting scheme of one or two types of plant that could be foliage on its own rather than eye-catching flowers, whereas plain containers benefit from more varied planting, which will draw the eye up away from the simplicity of the base. Large, plain containers also look good if surrounded by smaller ones. When setting up a display of pots it is important to ensure there is some unifying theme, otherwise the whole area can end up looking a bit of a hotchpotch. Similar shaped pots of different sizes displayed together look good and a variety of pots made of the same material – like terracotta – can look very effective. If you wish to group very different containers together you can unify them by sticking to one type of plant or by displaying a variety of plants in a single colour. If you are not satisfied with your display the first time, remember pots can be moved and often easily replanted.

Containers can also be used to create simple water features. Ready-made water features can be inexpensive to buy and many contain pumps and fountains that simply need connecting to the mains. As long as the inside is completely sealed, any container can be filled to make a raised pond.

Any object can be used to grow plants in as long as it is able to hold soil and will allow water to drain through it. An enormous variety of purpose-made containers are available from garden centres and antique salvage yards, from tiny plastic pots to antique urns costing vast sums of money. Apart from cost and size, your choice of containers may also be influenced by the style of your house and existing garden. Metal containers usually look good in minimalist, modern gardens whereas old stone or terracotta usually suits old houses and more traditional gardens. Before you buy containers, look at pictures in books and magazines or visit other gardens and decide what would suit your garden most. Also decide whether you want the pot or the plants in it to be the focal point. If the container itself is to be the main attraction on the patio, you will need to choose it very carefully. A pot covered by a mass of ivy and trailing plants need only be a cheap, plain one.

Terracotta

This is probably the most common material for constructing containers. It suits almost all situations and weathers attractively with age. Large terracotta pots are heavy, but this makes them stable and therefore less likely to blow over. Even if it has been fired to a high temperature, unglazed terracotta is nearly always slightly porous. This means water seeps through the container and can cause problems for two reasons. Firstly, the soil may tend to dry out. This is particularly noticeable in small pots, but can be overcome by lining the pot with plastic or placing a smaller plastic pot inside the terracotta one. If lining the pots, always remember to make plenty of drainage holes at the bottom. Water seeping into the terracotta in cold weather can cause the second problem – frost damage. When the water held

within the pot freezes, it expands and can cause the pot to crack or even shatter. Containers labelled frost-proof are less likely to suffer from this problem, but no terracotta pot can be 100 per cent frost-proof. In very severe winters it is better to bring your pots indoors or protect them with lagging (see section on winter care of containers). Glazed pots to do not suffer from moisture loss but are not always frost-proof.

Terracotta pots come in a great variety of shapes and sizes. Urn shapes with narrow necks can be hard to keep sufficiently watered, and large containers have a tendency to become soggy in winter so always ensure the drainage is as good as possible in these.

Stone and fake stone

Genuine antique stone containers can look amazing, but also tend to be extremely expensive and heavy to move. For most people fake stone is a much more practical option. It is made of a variety of concrete mixtures most of which are frost-proof and will age in the same way as real stone. This process can take up to five years, but will be speeded up considerably if you paint the surface with a coating of sour milk, yogurt or diluted manure.

Timber

All timber needs to be treated, otherwise it will eventually rot and fall apart. Every three to five years the container should be emptied, dried and treated with preservative or paint. For this reason it is often easier to plant up a plastic container and put it inside the wooden one so that the plants can be removed easily when necessary. Long troughs and window boxes are particularly suited to having the plants in a plastic inner container as it allows for seasonal variations. Alternatively you can line the timber container with polythene to protect it. This also ensures the container is waterproof. Barrels used for beer, etc. are sealed, but others may not be. Half barrels make extremely stable planters and are useful for windy sites where other containers might blow over. Square or rectangular wooden planters tend to look more formal and can be very effective if planted with formally shaped plants, such as trimmed box.

Plastic

This is the cheapest form of container and can look good if carefully positioned. An important factor to remember is that a bright terracotta pot will fade and mellow whereas a bright plastic pot never will. Plastic containers are also light and may need to be weighted down if in an exposed site. Although it is frost-proof, plastic becomes brittle if exposed to bright sunlight and will eventually crack. Having listed all the drawbacks of using plastic containers, it has to be said that they are invaluable as window boxes and on balconies and roof gardens where you do not want a heavy container. They are also useful as part of a temporary display and in situations where the pot is not actually visible.

Other materials

As stated earlier, anything that will hold soil and allow water to drain through it can be used as a container. A wicker basket, for example, may only last as a container for a season or two, but this will allow you to alter the garden rather than simply planting up the same annuals year after year. Before you throw away a leaking bucket or old watering can, check first whether it might look good planted up in the garden.

Lead containers can look beautiful, but tend to be very heavy and expensive. Fibreglass copies are frequently more practical and many are so good that you cannot tell they are fakes until you touch them.

Planting and care

Good drainage is one of the most important factors in successful container gardening and to facilitate this pots must *always* have drainage holes and should be raised off the ground to allow excess water to drain out of them. Terracotta 'feet' are available at most garden centres, or you can use bricks for larger pots. Very large containers that you wish to move around the garden can be put on a slatted wooded base with wheels. This allows drainage and enables the pot to be moved easily.

When you buy a container, always check it has enough drainage holes. They are marked on many plastic troughs, but not pushed out. This can easily be done with any sharp instrument. Holes of 0.5–1 cm (¼–½ in) every 10–12 cm (4–5 in) are probably adequate for most containers. If you are using a recycled object, like a tin bucket, remember you must make drainage holes in it before planting it up.

You must also ensure that the chosen site is strong enough to support the container. Remember that it will be much heavier when it is full of moist soil and may be unstable if it is in an exposed area. Also be careful when positioning it to ensure that the container is not dripped on by gutters or overhanging trees or other plants.

Large containers are best planted in situ, whereas smaller ones can be filled on a table or workbench. If you are planting up a plastic container that will sit inside something else, always plant it up inside the other pot as the sides of the plastic pot will sag outwards when it is full of soil. This is particularly important for window

simple black plastic pots have been used here as containers as the arch draws the eye upwards and away from them

cross-section of a planted container
at the bottom are crocks to help drainage
large bulbs can be put near the bottom of the container with smaller bulbs above
plants should be positioned so that temporary bedding plants can be removed without disturbing the permanent plants
you should leave a gap between the top of the pot and the surface of the compost otherwise any water will simply run off

boxes and long troughs. If you wish to insulate terracotta pots, you need to line them with polythene at this stage, making sufficient drainage holes in the bottom. Alternatively you can use strips of polystyrene or spray-on insulating foam which will do the same job.

Planting

First, put a layer of stones or broken crocks into the container. This layer must be deep enough to allow the water to soak through without allowing the soil to clog up the drainage holes. The depth will vary according to the size of the container, but 2.5–5 cm (1–2 in) is usually sufficient.

Next fill the container with soil. Always use fresh compost. However rich it looks do not be tempted to re-use old compost or garden soil as neither will have enough nutrients to support the growing plants in a container. Multi-purpose compost is fine for most containers but check for any particular requirements your chosen plants may have. If you wish to improve the drainage, you can mix in up to a quarter perlite or vermiculite. This will also allow the roots to move easily through the soil and will lessen the overall weight of the container.

Before you start putting in plants and bulbs, you must ensure that the soil in the container and around the plants going into it is moist. It is very important that it is not bone dry, but equally it should not be waterlogged. Plant up the container with large bulbs at the bottom, then smaller bulbs and finally surface plants following the instructions on p. 55. When planting you can also mix in bonemeal and slow-release fertilizer if you wish. A handful of bonemeal will be sufficient for a 45-cm (18-in) pot and slow-release fertilizer comes with instructions regarding the quantities you should use. The goodness in the compost will only last five to six weeks and after that you will have to provide food for the plants on a regular basis.

Plant up to within 1 cm (½ in) of the rim of the container. The soil will sink down leaving about 2.5 cm (1 in) at the top, which allows for a layer of mulch or grit. This looks attractive, prevents evaporation, stops weeds growing and deters slugs and snails. Even if you are not going to use a surface layer, always make sure there is a gap between the surface of the soil and the rim of the container as otherwise any water will simply run off, probably taking the soil with it.

Watering

Plants in containers need more water than those planted directly in the ground as their roots cannot spread out so far and more is lost through evaporation. It is possible to install an irrigation system but this is only really useful if you have a lot of pots or if they are situated on exposed balconies or roof gardens and dry out very quickly. Irrigation systems are also useful if you go away for long periods in the summer, but if this is the case you might be advised to plant your garden with fewer containers, and more drought-tolerant, soil-planted specimens. Watering your containers by hand allows you to judge exactly how much each one needs and to check on the plants as you go round. As a rough guideline, feel the soil 2.5 cm (1 in) below the surface – if it is dry you need to water. Moisture meters are available from garden centres but it is perfectly simple to test by hand.

Moisture-retaining granules can be added at the time of planting. The idea is that they swell up and retain water, which they then release as the soil dries out. It is important to remember that you still need to water – just not as often. Water slowly and gently using a hose or watering can and allow the water time to penetrate the soil properly. Once the soil is saturated, water will start to drain out of the bottom of the pot. If the water falls straight out through the drainage holes the minute you add it, this means the plant has dried out or become root bound, i.e. the roots have grown too large for the pot. In this case, soak the pot in a bucket with water half way up the pot's sides and leave it until all the bubbles have stopped rising to the surface. Then re-pot the plant in a larger container with plenty of soil to accommodate the roots.

It is also possible to water plants from the base by sitting them in a dish of water. This is a good method as it allows the plant to take up exactly the amount of water it needs, but you have to be careful as the dish will collect rainwater and the pot may become waterlogged. Dishes are particularly useful if you are going away for the summer. Put the containers close together in a shady, sheltered spot to minimize evaporation and stand the containers in dishes of water.

In winter be very careful not to over-water containers. Many plants are better able to withstand cold than damp.

Feeding

After about the first six weeks it will be necessary to provide food as well as water for your container plants. As a rough guide, supplements containing nitrogen will strengthen leaves and stems whereas potash will help to promote flowers and fruits. Phosphorous helps root development, and bonemeal, which is rich in phosphorous, added at planting time will get the plants off to a good start. A fortnightly feed of liquid seaweed during the growing time will often be sufficient. Tomato food encourages the growth of flowers and is very effective when given to annuals. Always follow the instructions on the container as too much food can do as much harm as too little. When feeding, it is important to

ensure the soil is moist throughout. If in any doubt, water well and feed the next day.

Winter care

Either the container or plant may be unable to withstand cold weather. Bear in mind that some plants, like olive trees, can put up with low temperatures but not a combination of cold winds and damp. Plants can be protected with sacking or straw wrapped round them or, if necessary, should be moved indoors. Often simply removing a container to a more sheltered spot may be sufficient. If you cannot do this and are worried about the container's frost hardiness, wrap it in bubblewrap, sacking or newspaper when temperatures below freezing are forecast.

Hanging baskets

Hanging baskets need slightly different treatment to other containers. They are usually made of wire mesh or plastic and are either free-hanging and circular or wall-mounted and semi-circular. It is worth buying the largest you can as the larger ones hold much more soil and do not dry out so fast. Depending on the size and situation of your basket, you will need to water it anything from twice a week to twice a day. If you are going away for any length of time, it is worth moving hanging baskets to a shady position.

To plant up, balance the basket in a bucket or against the back of a garden chair. You will need to provide some sort of lining to hold the soil in place. Sphagnum moss looks attractive and allows you to push plants through the base, coconut fibre mats can be cut to fit any basket or rigid liners made from recycled paper can be bought in most sizes. All are available from garden centres. Rigid liners are probably the least attractive, but the easiest to plant up and to a certain extent they can be disguised by encouraging trailing plants to hang over the edge of the basket. If using coconut fibre matting, cut and fold it to fit the basket and then cut holes where you wish to put trailing plants. Only make small holes (just large enough to push the plant through) otherwise the earth will fall out. For sphagnum moss, line the basket with moss to a depth of 4 cm (1½ in). Insert the trailing plants through the gaps in the basket and then add a layer of compost.

It is worth adding fertilizer and perlite or vermiculite to

it is easiest to plant up a hanging basket if you wedge it in the top of a bucket
push plants through the side of the basket as you work your way up, planting the top last
allow a gap of at least 3 cm (1 in) between the surface of the compost and the rim of the basket

the mixture to provide nutrients and lessen the weight. A handful of each will probably be sufficient for most hanging baskets. Add more trailing plants if you wish around the sides of the basket and then plant up the top. Push the soil down firmly and make sure there is at least one inch between the level of the soil and the rim of the basket to allow for watering.

Remember that once it is planted, the basket will be quite heavy so ensure its supports are strong enough. Try to avoid placing the hanging basket in a windy spot as wind dries out the soil even faster than sun.

Window boxes

These need to be planted up in the same way as any other container, but it should be done carefully as window boxes are normally very much on display. Remember

also that they need to look good from both inside the house and out. If you have wooden boxes with plastic linings you can remove one lining as soon as the plants start to fade and replace it with a new set of planting in a second lining. This method allows bulbs to die back naturally and also enables you to grow plants from seed in the containers before putting them into the wooden troughs. While they are out of use, the plastic liners can be kept in a less noticeable part of the garden. As the window box gets warmth from the house, it is possible to plant more tender plants than you could in an open site in the garden. As with all containers, make sure your window boxes have adequate drainage and are firmly secured in place.

Balconies and roof gardens

Before you put containers on a balcony or roof it is vital to find out how strong it is. Get an architect or structural engineer to check out the area for you and take into account the weight of the soil as well as of the containers.

Both areas will be subjected to strong winds and, depending on where the walls are, unnaturally high or low levels of sunlight. It is often worth putting up trellis as this will act as a windbreak but will not block out too much light. Climbers such as cup-and-saucer vines (*Cobaea scandens*) and morning glory (*Ipomoea purpurea*) can withstand considerable winds. Plastic or fibreglass containers are usually best except for tall plants, which will need a solid base to prevent them being blown over.

The warmth rising from the house and high levels of sunlight extend the growing season on roof gardens and enable you to grow a greater range of plants than you would be able to at ground level. Many plants of Mediterranean origin are suitable as they can withstand full sun, drought and, in most cases, strong winds.

Plants

Most containers are planted with a mixture of plant types such as perennials, bulbs, annuals and maybe a shrub. One or two types of plant require particular conditions and these are considered on the following pages.

Alpines

Alpines do particularly well in containers as it is possible to mimic the thin, well-drained soil that they are used to in their natural habitats. Any container with good drainage works well, but large sinks and stone troughs are particularly effective as they show off the little plants to great advantage. Rocks can also be added making the result look more natural. Put up to 10 cm (4 in) of pebbles or broken crocks in the bottom of the container to ensure really good drainage. In a shallow trough you will not have room for so much but allow about one-third crocks to two-thirds earth. On top of this put a layer of gravel and then the planting mixture which should be 50/50 grit and compost. Once you have planted up the container, add another layer of grit on the surface to deter slugs and snails. Try to give the container a really good soaking when it is dry, rather than watering little and often, as this will mimic the mountain storms that the plants thrive in. Below is a selection of alpines that are easy to grow.

Alyssum compactum (Tom Thumb)
Armeria (Thrift)
Aubretia
Campanula carpactica
C. garganica
Dianthus alpinus
D. freynii (Pinks)
Dryas minor octopetala
Gentiana verna
Geranium cinereum (Cranesbill)
Helianthemum innulatum (Rock rose)
Lewisia cotyledon
Phlox sublata
P. douglasii
Saxifraga
Sedum canticolum (Stonecrop)
Sempervivum
Viola biflora
V. gracili
V. lutea

Perennials

These are not as commonly used in containers as annuals and shrubs. Most have a dormant period when they die down or need to be cut back and do not look so attractive during this time. However, they can be useful in large containers to form part of a year-round planting scheme where other plants, such as shrubs or bulbs, are designed to provide interest while the perennials are dormant. Below some perennials are listed that can be successfully grown in containers.

Agapanthus (African lily)
Alchemilla mollis (Lady's mantle)
Astilbe
Bergenia
Dicentra (Bleeding heart)
Geranium (Cranesbill)
Geum
Helleborus niger (Christmas rose)
H. orientalis (Lenten rose)
Hemerocallis (Day lily)
Hosta
Sedum spectabile (Ice plant)
Stachys lanata (Lambs' ears)

Bulbs

All bulbs will do well in containers and can be densely planted as long as you provide sufficient nutrients and water. Bulbs are very useful in containers since they can provide flowers from late winter to early summer. Any varieties of the following are worth growing.

Chionodoxa (Glory-of-the-snow)
Crocus
Cyclamen
Fritillaria
Gallanthus (Snowdrop)
Iris
Lilium (Lily)
Muscari (Grape hyacinth)
Narcissi (Daffodil)
Tulipa (Tulip)

Grasses

Grasses are very good specimen plants and a single grass may be all you need in a particularly ornate container. Chosen carefully, they can be designed to form the main attraction of the container while any perennials are lying dormant. The following list includes sedges, but all will do well in containers.

Carex riparia (Sedge)
C. elata (Sedge)
Festuca glauca
Hakonechloa macra

Helictotrichon sempervirens
Imperator cylindrica
Miscanthus sinensis
Molinia caerulea
Phalaris arundinacea

Shrubs

Many shrubs will grow perfectly happily in containers although not all will reach their full size. Ideally the container should be a quarter to a third as tall as the final height of the plant and roughly the same diameter. You should use John Innes number 3 or specialist tree and shrub compost as this will provide the necessary nutrients to get the plant started. You will need to feed during the growing season and water as necessary throughout the year as most shrubs do not have such a noticeable dormant period as perennials. Climbers can also be grown successfully in containers, but the container should be as large as possible to allow maximum growth. Below is a selection of shrubs and climbers that can be grown successfully in containers.

Shrubs

Azalea
Arundinaria japonica (Bamboo)
Berberis thunbergii
Buxus sempervirens (Box)
Camellia japonica williamsii
Choisya (Mexican orange)
Convolvulus cneorum (Shrubbery bindweed)
Euonymus fortunei or *radicans*
E. japonicus
Fatsia japonica
Hebe
Hydrangea
Lavendula (Lavender)
Patio roses
Pieris
Ribes
Viburnum
Vinca major or *minor* (Periwinkle)
Weigela

Climbers

Clematis armandii florida
Hedera helix (Ivy)
Parthenocissus (Virginia creeper)
Vitis (Vine)
Wisteria

Trees

Various trees can be grown in containers but most will not reach their full size and will not live as long as they would if planted in the ground. It is important to water trees in containers regularly and to ensure that the water penetrates right to the bottom of the container. The best way to do this is to water the tree once a week with a lot of water so the soil is really soaked rather than giving it a little every day. Ideally the container should be a minimum of 50 cm (20 in) deep and wide. When planting, use specialist tree and shrub compost and allow 8 cm (3 in) between the surface of the soil and the edge of the pot. This gap will allow you to soak the plant thoroughly when you water it. The water will then penetrate the entire pot and the excess will drain away through the bottom. If cared for, the following trees will all do well in pots.

Acer plamatum negundo (Maple)
Citrus limon (Lemon)
Citrus sinensis (Orange)
Gunnii (Eucalyptus)
Ilex aquifolium (Holly)
Lauris noblis (Sweet bay)
Olea europea (Olive)
Prunus (Flowering cherry)
Salix caprea pendula (Willow)

Citrus and olive trees are best grown in pots as they can be moved indoors or to a more sheltered spot during the winter.

Herbs

All herbs can be grown in containers and in fact many do better grown in this way as it is easier to provide the well-drained soil they like and thereby prevent them from becoming waterlogged. Mint is always best grown in a container as it is highly invasive. See the herb section on p. 110 for cultivation.

Fruit

Many compact varieties of fruit trees are now available and these can be successfully grown in containers. Apple, cherry, fig, peach and plum are all possibilities, fig being particularly suitable as it grows best when its roots are constricted. Currant and gooseberry bushes can be grown in containers, but the most successful container fruits of all are strawberries. You can even acquire a specially designed pot to grow them in. Strawberry pots curve upwards gently and have openings up the sides. This enables you to grow plants all over the pot and gives the strawberries the maximum chance to reach the sun and ripen.

Vegetables

Many vegetables can be grown in containers and you can buy growing bags especially for this purpose. The bags are not particularly attractive, but the foliage of some plants, such as courgettes, will quickly grow to hide them or alternatively you could place a row of low containers in front of the bags. Cultivation of vegetables is covered in Chapter 10, but carrots, courgettes, cucumbers, French beans, runner beans, ruby chard and tomatoes all do particularly well in containers.

Planting schemes

The variety of combinations of plants that could be put in containers is almost endless. There are no rigid rules and given sufficient care virtually any plant will grow in a container. There are, however, one or two guidelines that are worth bearing in mind when planting up a container:

1. If the container itself is very beautiful, there is no point covering it with trailing plants. A single upright specimen is often more effective.

2. Conversely unattractive pots can usually be hidden beneath trailing ivies and flowers, such as trailing *Lobelia*, nasturtiums or trailing petunias.

3. There is a fine dividing line between a brilliant riot of colour and a disarray of ill-matched plants.

4. Different plants of the same colour usually look good, e.g. a variety of different plants all with blue flowers or bluey-green foliage.

5. Similar plants in contrasting colours can be effective, e.g. red and green, blue and orange and purple and yellow.

6. Look at the position where your container will live and make sure it blends well with its surroundings. If it is meant to be the dominant feature of an area, make sure it really does stand out and is not overshadowed by surrounding plants or features.

this urn is an attractive ornament and looks best filled with upright plants that do not hide it

On the following pages are lists of plants that perform various useful functions. Bear in mind that the lists are *not* comprehensive. They are only there to give you a few ideas to get you started.

Spring

The trick is to plant the bulbs fairly deeply so that you can put a layer of annuals or perennials above them. Put the biggest and later-flowering bulbs at the bottom and this will give you a longer flowering period.

Bulbs
Chionodoxa
Crocus
Cyclamen
Fritillaria
Galanthus (Snowdrop)
Iris
Lilium (Lily)
Muscari (Grape hyacinth)
Narcissi (Daffodil)
Tulipa (Tulip)

Annuals and perennials
Bellis perennis (Daisy)
Erysimum cheiri syn *Cheiranthus* (Wallflower)
Helleborus
Myosotis (Forget-me-not)
Primula
Viola

Shrubs and trees
Camellia
Magnolia stellata
Prunus (Flowering cherry)

Summer

In many ways this is the easiest season for containers as most annuals are in flower during this time.

Flowers
Alchemilla mollis (Lady's mantle)
Alyssum
Antirrhinum (Snapdragon)
Argyranthemum fructens (Marguerite)
Fuchsias
Helichrysum petiolare
Impatiens (Busy Lizzies)
Lobelia
Nicotiana (Tobacco plant)
Osteospermum
Pelargoniums
Petunia
Tropaeolum (Nasturtium)
Verbena

Shrubs
Buddleja
Ceanothus
Choisya (Mexican orange)
Hebe
Hibiscus
Jasminium officinale (Summer jasmine)

Autumn
Flowers
Ajuga reptans
Antirrhinum (Snapdragon)
Dendranthema (Chrysanthemum)
Lamium maculatum
Matthiola (Stock)
Viola (Pansy)

Shrubs and trees
Acer palmatum (Maple)
Ceratostigma
Fuchsia
Hibiscus
Hydrangea

Winter
Flowers and other plants
Carex (Sedge)
Hedera (Ivy)
Helleborus niger (Christmas rose)
Miscantus sinensis (Ornamental grass)
Ornamental kale
Polypodium vulgare (Ornamental fern)
Vinca
Viola (Pansy)

Shrubs and trees
Berberis
Buxus (Box)
Pieris
Skimmia
Viburnum

Hanging baskets

Alyssum
Calendula (Marigold)
Fuchsia
Hedera (Ivy)
Heliotropum (Heliotrope)

Impatiens (Busy Lizzies)
Lobelia
Minimulus (Monkey flower)
Osteospermum
Pelargonium
Petunia
Verbena
Tropaeolum (Nasturtium)
Viola (Pansy)

Scented plants
Flowers
Aloysia triphylla (Lemon verbena)
Chamaemelum nobile (Chamomile)
Convallaria majalis (Lily-of-the-valley)
Cosmos
Dianthus (Pinks)
Dianthus Barbatus (Sweet william)
Freesia
Hyacinthus
Lathyrus odoratus (Sweet pea)
Lilium regale (Lily)
Matthiola bicomis (Night-scented stock)
Mignonette
Nicotiana (Tobacco plant)

Shrubs
Jasminium officinale (Jasmine)
Lavendulus (Lavender)
Rosa (Rose)
Rosmarinus (Rosemary)

Plants suitable for shade
Flowers
Convallaria majalis (Lily-of-the-valley)
Fuchsia
Hedera (Ivy)
Hosta
Impatiens (Busy Lizzies)
Mimulus (Monkey flower)
Nicotiana (Tobacco plant)
Viola (Pansy)

Shrubs
Azalea
Buxus (Box)
Camellia
Choisya (Mexican orange)
Conifers
Euonymus
Fatsia
Vinca

69 courtyard and patio gardens

A patio may form part of a larger garden or take up the whole area of a small one. Courtyards, as they are largely enclosed, tend to be separate from any other areas of the garden. If you are building a patio as part of an existing garden, it is most important to site it correctly. In many gardens the most practical place is near the house, but consider other options – it may be nice to walk down a path and either sit in a totally secluded area or look back at the house. Either way, ensure the patio is easily accessible and well lit if you are considering sitting out on it in the evening. Take into account when you will most use the patio and whether you want it to be in the sun or the shade.

If the patio is part of a larger garden, it is important that it fits in with the overall design. It should either blend in with the house or provide a sharp contrast. Links can easily be achieved by matching the construction material or even by echoing the paint colour of the house in the garden furniture.

When designing a patio from scratch, always make it as large as possible. You need to be able to fit a table and chairs on it and still allow room to walk round. If you find it is too large, you can always fill it up with some big containers. If the patio joins directly to the lawn, make the level slightly lower than the grass as this will make mowing much easier.

If the garden has already got a patio, you can alter it to a certain extent by adding containers or raised beds. The edges can also be softened or modified by planting round

the patio. If you do not initially like the position, wait a few months before you move it – the previous owners may have had a logical reason for siting it where they did, such as getting the evening sun, etc. If the patio you inherit is very dirty and covered with moss and algae, remove what you can with a stiff broom and then wash using soapy water. Use any chemical cleaners with care and be sure that they do not soak into the surrounding soil.

If you have a small garden, it is often better to turn the whole area into a patio rather than having a lawn. Narrow beds round the edge of the patio garden, with a mixture of tall and short plants, will give you a greater sense of space, particularly if you can fit in a couple of rows of graduated heights. For small gardens, privacy is often an important aspect and trellises with climbers can be very useful as they do not take up as much room as a hedge and do not block out as much light as a tall fence or wall. A good combination is to have a fence or wall up to 1.6–1.8 m (5–6 ft) and then trellis on top. An arbour or pergola will also provide privacy and a certain amount of shade depending how thickly you train the plants over it. Small city gardens can be dark, but if you grow a variety of climbers you can create interest without losing too much light. Carefully positioned lighting can also make a great difference to the appearance of a small garden.

Enclosed gardens or courtyards can be very sheltered and you may find that you can grow a greater range of plants than you would be able to on a more exposed site in the same area.

a simple urn surrounded by spring bulbs can provide a splash of colour beside a patio
the plants could easily be changed as the year progresses to provide seasonal interest

Be careful with the design of a small patio garden – when working on a small scale every detail is important. In large gardens it is often possible to disguise unattractive features, such as an old shed, while in a small garden any fault will tend to stand out. Most styles can be adapted to a small garden and, within reason, most features. Formal water features usually work better in small spaces and the sound of flowing water can greatly enhance the peace of a city patio garden. If you want to plant a tree, bear in mind what its roots may do to surrounding buildings and where it will cast shadows. Small trees such as *Acer palmatum* (Japanese maple), *Malus robusta* (Crab apple), *Sorbus* (Mountain ash), *Crataegus* Paul's Scarlet (Hawthorn) or *Prunus* (Flowering cherry or almond) are all suitable.

Trellis, mirrors or even *trompe-l'oeil* can create the illusion of a greater area of garden, but these features must be positioned very carefully to be effective. Always try to position mirrors so that they reflect part of the garden rather than the people in it. You want to create the impression of more space, rather than more people!

Materials

In any patio or courtyard, regardless of size, the most important element in terms of basic design is the material of which it is made. Plants can be moved or altered, but the feel of the area will be largely determined by what material you use as its base since this will form the backdrop for everything else. The main materials available for this use are listed below, together with their pros and cons:

Natural stone

This group includes stones such as York stone and sandstone. Most look very good, particularly if they echo the stone of surrounding buildings. The downsides are that they tend to be expensive, heavy and can be slippery when wet.

Paving slabs

A huge variety is available, ranging from good imitations of natural stone to cheap slabs. They also come in a great variety of shapes including hexagonal, octagonal and circular. If creating a pattern, be careful to what extent it stands out – the use of greatly contrasting colours can be very dominating. Take care when buying pre-cast slabs. Although they are often very cheap, they can also be very brittle and break easily.

Concrete

This is versatile and can be used to infill most spaces, but can look dull and is usually better if used in conjunction with another material, such as brick edging.

Bricks

These can look lovely but are dark and therefore not always suitable for a small shady garden. They can be laid in interesting patterns, such as herringbone, and set to fit most shaped areas. If you are planning an area, make sure you have enough similar bricks as different types will stand out unattractively.

Slate

This can look interesting, but tends to be dark and dominating. It can also be very slippery when wet.

Decking

Hardwood decking is very versatile and combines particularly well with gravel, plants and water. The wood must be well treated and can be prone to slipperiness and rot. To a certain extent the danger of slipping can be reduced by covering the area with fine chicken-wire nailed down at regular intervals. A great variety of natural colours and patterns is available. Use these to create interest as a large area of identical planks all going the same way can look very monotonous.

Gravel, pebbles and granite sets

All these surfaces tend to be too uneven for patios if you intend to use the area for eating. They are more suited to paths and areas that are not used for seating and therefore do not need to be completely level.

Use of mortar

The final question is whether to mortar in between the stones. If you do use mortar, no weeds should get through, but you will have to be careful that any water runs off the surface rather than collecting in unattractive pools. Sand placed around the stones will create a firm surface, but will not deter all weeds. If you leave slightly larger gaps between the stones or even omit some stones altogether you can grow plants around the paving stones, which will soon establish themselves and deter any weeds.

Plants for crevices

Campanula carpactica
C. cochlearifolia (Fairy's thimbles)
C. portenschalagiana
C. poscharskyana
Lobelia erinus
Lobularia maritima (Sweet alyssum)
Menta requienii
Nemophilia maculata (Five spots)
N. menziesii (Baby blue eyes)
Sedum kamtschaticum
S. spathulifolium
Thymus (Thyme)

Paths

Unless your garden is entirely made up of a patio, you will need paths of some sort. Apart from being practical, paths can add interest to the garden and curved paths can be used to make a small garden look larger by giving the impression that they wind away to another area that is out of sight. Even if you do not have such an area, you can always create a focal point towards which your path can lead, such as a statue, a fountain or an urn of flowers. These are all features that should fit easily into any garden, however small.

The choice of materials for a path is much the same as for a patio, although, because it does not need to be as flat, gravel or cobbles could be used as well. Before laying a path, think carefully about who will use it – small children and wheelchair users will need wide, level paths, as will people carrying food to a patio or barbecue. On the other hand a path to encourage interest or protect the lawn in winter can simply consist of stepping stones. When laying stepping stones, always be sure it is easy to step from one to the next, otherwise people will simply ignore them and trample on the lawn or plants in between.

When laying a path, think about the effect you want to create. Bricks laid endways, for example, will encourage people to walk along the path, whereas laid horizontally they discourage movement and would be more suited to a patio or the area at the end of the path. As with patios, paths are best laid below the level of the grass but above the flowerbed, unless you have completely solid edging.

Edging

Specially made edgings can be bought from most garden centres. They can range from traditional rope-edged tiles to patterned concrete in a variety of shapes and colours. Metal options range from old-fashioned iron to modern stainless steel. Treated wood is also a good material to use. Solid railway timbers will act as boundaries for your flowerbeds and contain the soil. Bamboo fencing or low hurdles will define the edge of the bed and possibly support plants but will not stop the soil from spilling out. Many styles of edging are also available in plastic, which is cheap, and although not necessarily very strong can look just as good as the original material. You do not need to restrict yourself to purpose-built edging – bricks laid diagonally on their sides form excellent boundaries as do roof tiles, which have the advantage of being thinner and therefore taking up less soil space. In fact anything that is flat and reasonably firm can be used – shells look lovely as long as the bed is not disturbed much as they do not hold soil back well. Natural edging can also be used in the form of box hedging or low-growing plants, such as thyme.

Furniture and ornaments

The final important thing to consider for a patio is the style of furniture and ornaments you want, if any. As with containers, it is important that they should either blend with the rest of the garden or make a carefully planned statement. Anything brightly coloured or white will stand out, whereas green or black will blend with the garden. This also applies to trellis and plant supports in general. White will also make everything around it seem brighter, but it is important for this effect that it is a clean white and not a dirty cream with patches of green mould!

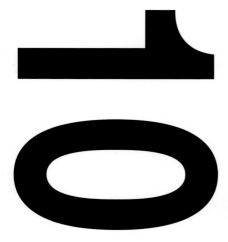

the kitchen garden

Whatever the size of your garden, you can grow your own produce. Window boxes are ideal for a small herb garden, tomatoes can be cultivated in grow-bags and more or less anything can flourish in a suitable container. If you really want to grow your own garden produce, then nothing should stop you. Many people derive enormous satisfaction from taking something directly from the garden to the table, but bear in mind that producing fruit and vegetables is much harder work than growing flowers. They require considerably more care and attention and you will therefore need a lot more time at your disposal to become a successful home produce gardener. It used to be the case that you could grow superior and cheaper produce in your own garden, but with the increase of farmers' markets and the general availability of organic produce, this is no longer necessarily so. It is not all hard work, however. There are many fruits, vegetables and herbs that can be grown reasonably easily and these will reward you handsomely for your efforts.

You can grow your edible plants either in amongst your flowers or in a specially designated vegetable patch. To some extent this will depend on the size of your garden and the priority you want to give to your home produce.

Herbs usually do better in an area specially set aside for them since they need very well-drained soil and a sunny position. Many varieties of fruit and vegetable, on the other hand, do well in flowerbeds and can look very attractive. You could even reverse the balance and have a vegetable garden with some flowers dotted in between

the produce. Potagers (French for vegetable garden) are ornamental gardens of fruit and vegetables laid out in intricate patterns, which can look very striking. Probably the most famous example is Villandry in France where the garden around the château is mainly full of fruit and vegetables. The ornamental possibilities of edible plants are endless. Fruit trees can be trained into attractive fans to decorate walls, beans and raspberries are good climbers and many salad crops have interesting foliage.

Planning your site

If you decide to set aside an area for your garden produce, you need to choose it carefully. Your plants will not thrive if they are stuck away in an exposed, shady corner of the garden. Herbs in particular are usually best grown near the house so that you have easy access to them while you are cooking. A collection of containers around the back door can be both attractive and practical.

The site you choose must be sunny and sheltered. This is the reason why walled kitchen gardens are traditionally found in large country house gardens. Having chosen your site you then need to plan it out carefully. The best method is usually to divide the area into sections so that you can grow plants with similar requirements in the same area.

This will also enable you to adopt a simple scheme of crop rotation, which is useful for growing vegetables.

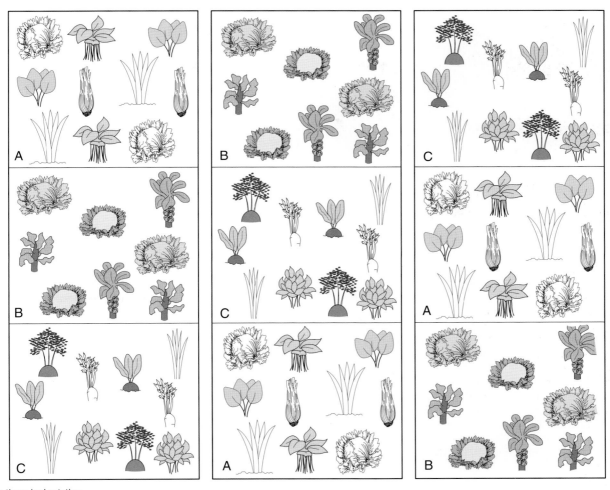

simple three-bed rotation

a: legumes, e.g. peas and beans, can be planted with celery, courgettes, leeks, lettuce, marrows, onions, spinach and tomatoes

b: brassicas such as broccoli, Brussels sprouts, cabbage, calabrese, cauliflower and kale

c: root vegetables, such as beetroot, carrots, parsnips and potatoes

Apart from strawberries, fruits grow on plants with woody stems which, like shrubs, need to stay in a permanent place. Vegetables are mostly annuals, growing from to seed to product in one year, so by a process of crop rotation you can grow the plants in a different place each year, which is both beneficial to the soil and helps prevent disease becoming established. The vegetable area should be divided into three and each section then planted out with one family type – legumes (peas and beans), brassicas (broccoli, cabbage, cauliflower and Brussels sprouts) and root crops (carrots, parsnips and

potatoes). Before working out the rotation system you should consider what you want to grow – there is no point devoting a third of your vegetable garden to cabbage if you do not particularly like it. Potatoes can be grown with the other root crops, or, if you want a lot you can devote a whole section to them. The main advantage of yearly rotation is that the soil never gets depleted. Brassicas benefit as they need the nitrogen that is released into the soil by the legumes. The root crops break up the soil and prevent it becoming compacted. Quick-growing plants, like salad crops and onions, can be grown in

an extensive variety of vegetables can be grown in most gardens

between the legumes. One thing you must do is keep a record each year of what you have planted where so you know exactly how to rotate them. It is worth doing this anyway so that you know which crops did well and which ones you particularly enjoyed growing and eating.

When planning the site, look carefully at where the sun falls at different times of the day and ensure that the plants that need the most sun, like tomatoes, are sited in the best position. Remember to allow for the fact that tall plants, such as currants or beans, will cast shadows.

Ideally, each bed should be surrounded by a path so that you can work without treading on the soil and compacting it. The size of each bed will be determined by how far you can reach – if the width of the bed is twice your stretch, you will be able to reach all parts of it from one side or the other. The paths should be at least 30 cm (1 ft) wide and some of them should be wide enough to take a wheelbarrow. Many people like to grow their fruit and vegetables in raised beds surrounded by timber and railway sleepers can be good for such a purpose. In this way the beds are easy to work as you do not have to bend so far and the raised height encourages them to warm up much more quickly in the spring.

Containers

Herbs grow particularly well in containers and many fruits and vegetables can also be successfully grown in this way. Specialist growing bags are available for many vegetables and although these are not usually very pretty to look at they can easily be disguised. The foliage of crops, like courgettes, will hide them anyway and you can always put a row of low containers in front with herbs or annuals in them. Tomatoes, beans, lettuce,

potatoes, courgettes and carrots will all do well in containers, but the containers must be deep to accommodate the roots of the vegetables. As with all container-grown plants, they will need regular feeding and watering.

Most fruits need large containers in order to flourish (see the section on trees and shrubs in containers on p. 90) and need a lot of care and attention. Strawberries are the exception. They thrive when grown in compact containers and even have pots designed specifically for this purpose.

Problems

The pests and diseases that attack the kitchen garden need to be taken more seriously than those that affect the flower garden. Your roses will probably survive and continue to bloom even if they have greenfly, but if pests devour your crops you will have nothing left to eat! For obvious reasons it is not really a good idea to spray your potential crops with chemicals. The best method of dealing with pests and disease is really just to keep a close eye on your plants so that you can spot any problems early on. You can net fruit bushes to prevent birds from eating the fruit, remove diseased parts of the plant as soon as they appear and remedy any nutritional deficiencies that become apparent.

Vegetables

Vegetables need a lot of care and attention but will repay you handsomely for your time and effort. Within a few months a packet of seeds can be transformed into a tasty meal. Vegetables do well in most soils, but they need a sunny site. As discussed at the beginning of this chapter, you can either allocate a particular piece of your garden to be used as your vegetable patch, where you can rotate the crops each year, or you can scatter the vegetables in among your flowers in general beds.

Vegetables fall into four main categories:

Leaf and salad
This includes cabbages, lettuce and rocket, as well as decorative varieties such as kale and ruby chard.

Fruiting and flowering
This category includes brassicas, like broccoli and

cauliflower, the cucurbit family, from Central and South America, of tomatoes, cucumbers, squashes, pumpkins and courgettes, and many other interesting and attractive plants including cardoons, aubergines, peppers and sweetcorn. Some vegetables in this category are perennials, like asparagus and globe artichokes, and these plants will need permanent beds. Note that cucurbits dislike frost and will need protection during cold months.

Podded
Peas and beans fall into this category and are useful as they grow vertically and therefore take up little ground space. Many of these plants flower attractively, for example, some runner beans have bright-red flowers in early summer.

Bulb, stem and root
Onions, garlic, potatoes, carrots, leeks and asparagus are the most common vegetables included in this group. Many of these plants do not look particularly attractive above ground, but they form the basic stock of a standard vegetable garden.

Sowing and planting
With a little careful planning, you will be able to enjoy fresh vegetables throughout the year. It is possible to extend the growing season of many vegetables by providing protection from cold and wind. You can use traditional cloches or polytunnel to protect the seedlings early on. Polytunnels need circular hoops every 30 cm (1 ft) and should be fixed at each end round a stake. Perforated sheets of plastic or fleeces can be gently draped over the plants and weighted down at the edges. With all these methods remember to allow adequate ventilation for the plant.

As most vegetables are annuals, you can choose new varieties to grow each year. Always keep a record of any vegetable you grow, how you treated it, how well it did and how tasty it was. This may seem a bore at the time, but the information will be invaluable when you come to plant the following year's seeds. New strains are being developed all the time – check the seed packet for the exact details of the plants and always try to plant disease-resistant varieties. You are bound to have some problems with diseases, but the resistant strains will greatly reduce this.

Companion planting
Companion planting can be an effective method to use against pests and diseases. Many plants unwittingly benefit others by deterring pests or helping to combat disease. Others help by improving the soil. Below is a chart showing which plants go well together and which combinations should be avoided. On page 102 there is a list of plants that are generally useful throughout the garden.

Companion planting

Crop	Good combination	Bad combination
Beans	Spinach, brassicas	Onions, garlic, sunflowers
Brassicas	Parsley, chrysanthemums	Onions, garlic, rue, strawberries
Carrots	Onions, garlic, rosemary, sage, chives, lettuce, tomatoes, radishes	
Courgettes	Sweetcorn, peas, beans	Potatoes, brassicas
Lettuce	Carrots, strawberries	
Onions	Carrots, brassicas, tomatoes, leeks, lettuce, chamomile	Beans
Peas	Beans, carrots, leeks, turnips, parsley, herbs generally	Onions, garlic
Potatoes	Beans, marigolds, strawberries	Tomatoes, apples, sunflowers, cucurbits, raspberries, strong herbs
Radishes	Chervil, nasturtiums, lettuce, peas	Brassicas, spinach
Tomatoes	French marigolds, basil, carrots, onions, garlic, nasturtiums, parsley, nettles	Brassicas, potatoes, fennel

Against cabbage white: basil, borage, hyssop, sage, rosemary, thyme.

Against aphids: onions, nasturtiums, spearmint, stinging nettles.

Against whitefly: nasturtium, French marigolds.

Against couchgrass: turnips.

Against weeds in general: lupins.

Nitrogen fixers: clover, lupins, leguminous plants.

on tomato plants pinch out any extra shoots that grow at the point where the side branches meet the main stem

when the plant reaches the height you want, pinch out the top

Planting distances

You should always read the information on seed packets carefully, but if you wish you can sometimes adapt the planting distances to fit the ground you have available. If space is limited, you can frequently plant the seeds much closer than the packet specifies, as long as you provide adequate food and water. Another method of space-saving is intercropping.

Intercropping

This method allows you to grow two crops in one space. Alternate fast and slow-growing crops and you will be able to harvest the first crop before the second has grown up. Lettuces and radishes in between carrots and parsnips are good examples of this.

Cut-and-come-again

This is a method designed to help you increase your yield. Some vegetables will sprout again when you cut the leaves off the first time. Examples include some lettuces and spinach, which will resprout as long as you leave 2.5 cm (1 in) of stem.

Watering

While the vegetables are growing, it is very important that they receive a regular supply of water. Without adequate water, many vegetables will have a tendency to bolt. This means that the plant, anticipating a drought, speeds up its growth and produces its flowers and seeds in order to complete its life cycle as quickly as possible. Clearly to maximize the yield of your plants you want to prolong their growing period as long as you can.

Weeding

A final word of warning regarding vegetables is weeding. When the new seedlings first appear they will be very delicate and you must keep the area they are grown in weed free. At first you will need to do this by hand, but as the crop grows you can simply hoe the weeds as they appear. Remember that weeds may grow faster than your vegetables and will take up valuable space as well as using up nutrients in the soil.

The following chart shows a selection of vegetables that are all fairly easy to grow. Do not be put off if something you want to grow is not included – not many vegetables are particularly difficult to grow and the important thing is to cultivate ones that you like.

Vegetables: planting, care and harvesting

Vegetables	Planting	Care	Harvesting	Problems	Notes
Broccoli and calabrese	Sunny site and moist soil. Plant seeds in trays or beds mid-spring and transplant early–mid-summer 60 cm (24 in) apart. Stagger planting to give crops in autumn and winter.	Water well, weed and feed after first head has been harvested. Sprouting broccoli may need earth built up around its stem as it get top heavy.	Cut central head first and then smaller side heads as they grow. These will get very small towards the end of the season.	Cabbage root fly, club root, caterpillars, birds.	Calabrese should be planted in situ two to three seeds 15 cm (6 in) apart and thinned. Romanesco is particularly good.
Broad beans	Well-manured, heavy soil but not waterlogged. Sow late winter onwards 3–5 cm (1½–2 in) deep, 23 cm (9 in) apart.	Do not allow to dry out once flowers have formed. Provide support.	Summer. Harvest when still small and beans just show through pods	Aphids.	Dwarf do best under glass. Longpods and Windsor are hardier and have more flavour. aquadulce claudia can be sown in late autumn for early spring crop.
Carrots	Sunny, sheltered site with deep, light soil. Sow in mid-spring once temperature is 7 °C (43 °F). Mix with sand and sow thinly in drills 15 cm (6 in) apart. Sow seeds in situ 7.5 cm (3 in) apart.	Weed and water gently. Feed when seedlings appear.	Summer to mid-winter. Pull up by hand or with a fork. Mulch in winter to keep soil malleable.	Carrot fly.	Avoid thinning as this encourages carrot fly. Interplant with onions to deter carrot fly.
Courgettes (Zucchini)	Sunny, sheltered site. Sow once soil is warm in late spring–early summer 13 °C (56 °F) 90 cm (3 ft) apart.	Feed every two weeks and water well when flowers appear. Too much water before will only encourage large leaves.	Mid-summer–late autumn. Best when 10 cm (4 in) long.	Aphids and slugs.	Fruits will wither if they do not have enough food and water.
French beans	Rich soil, sheltered sunny site. Sow seeds in situ 22 cm (9 in) apart. Sow late spring once soil is 12 °C (54 °F) up to mid-summer.	Provide support. Mulch to avoid weeds. Water well, especially when flowering.	Mid-summer to mid-autumn. Pick when 10 cm (4 in) long. For haricot beans, leave on pod, cut whole plant when all pods are grown and dry indoors.	Slugs, black bean aphid and red spider mite. Grey mould in damp conditions.	Purple, yellow and green varieties available. Dwarf types can be fiddly to pick.
Lettuce	Good drainage, sun or partial shade. Sow 1 cm (½ in) deep. Thin when seedlings appear and again after four weeks. Sow at ten-day intervals.	Feed every three to four weeks. Weed well. Water in morning so leaves can dry and avoid mildew.	Can eat second thinning. Harvest regularly as they do not keep once ripe. Earliest crop ready in four weeks.	Aphids, slugs, birds. Bolting or tip burn due to lack of water.	Types available for most seasons. Can grow lettuce all year. Choose strains resistant to grey mould.

continued

Vegetables: planting, care and harvesting – *continued*

Vegetables	Planting	Care	Harvesting	Problems	Notes
Onions	Fertile soil, good drainage and sun. Plant sets so tops are just visible 10 cm (4 in) apart in spring. Seeds can be grown in trays and transplanted or in situ, early–mid-spring.	Push sets back into soil if lifted by birds. Weed and water if dry.	Ready when leaves dry and bend over. Early autumn onwards.	Onion fly.	Sets are better in areas of poor soil. Mature quicker and do not get onion fly but cost more and limited range.
Peas	Moist soil, sun or partial shade. Sow in situ early spring to mid-summer, using early, second early and then maincrop types.	Grow up framework of pea sticks. Mulch. Feed at seedling stage and water well when in flower.	Pick at regular intervals to encourage growth.	Net against birds. Mice. Plant strains resistant to mildew and fusarium wilt.	Wrinkle seeded varieties sweeter but less hardy. Grow smooth seeded varieties early and late in season.
Potatoes	Moist, slightly acidic soil. Dig manure or compost before planting. Leave on trays indoors in cool, light place to sprout. Plant one month before last frost. 10 cm (4 in) deep, 30 cm (12 in) apart with 60 cm (24 in) between rows.	Water, feed plants when young and pile up earth round base as necessary. Potatoes must not come above ground.	Earlies planted early to mid-spring, crop early to mid-summer. Maincrop planted mid-spring, will crop mid-autumn. Second earlies in between. Dig up whole plant gently with fork.	Potato scab due to too little water. Potato blight – grow resistant types or first earlies. Eelworms.	Only use specially developed seed potatoes, others could have diseases. Earlies and second earlies mature faster, maincrop slower (15, 17 and 19 weeks respectively).
Radishes	Light soil, partial shade. Sow 1 cm (½ in) deep, 15 cm (6 in) apart. Sow at two-week intervals between early spring and early autumn.	Water regularly.	Late spring onwards. Winter varieties mature more slowly (mid-summer to mid-winter).	Slugs.	Oval shapes in red, green, black, purple and yellow. Mooli and daikon are long, white and are winter varieties.
Rocket, Roquette, Rugola, Arugola	Any soil, partial shade. Sow every two weeks from early spring to late summer. Thin seedlings to 15 cm (6 in) apart.	Water, weed and feed regularly.	Cut leaves 3 cm (1½ in) above soil and new leaves will grow.		Edible rocket is *Eruca vesicaria* ssp *sativa*. Do not confuse with sweet rocket *Hesperis matronalis*.

continued

Vegetables	Planting	Care	Harvesting	Problems	Notes
Runner beans	Moist soil, full sun or partial shade. Compost soil well. Sow in late spring when soil is 10 °C (50 °F). Sow in pairs 15 cm (6 in) apart.	Provide support, feed at seedling stage, mulch and water well especially when in flower.	Late summer to mid-autumn. Pick when 10–15 cm (4–6 in) long.	Slugs, black bean aphid, red spider mite and pollen beetles.	Tall, dwarf and stringless varieties available.
Tomatoes	Fertile soil and sheltered sunny site. South-facing wall is ideal. Sow seeds indoors early to mid-spring. Harden and plant outside when soil is 10 °C (50 °F). Cordons 38–45 cm (15–18 in) apart and bushes 45–60 cm (18–24 in) apart.	Mulch. Water but not too much as fruit can split (11 litres or 2 gallons per week once flowers appear). Feed with specialist tomato food following instructions. Pinch out side shoots and top shoot of cordons when at the height you want. (See diagram p. 102.)	Remove ripe fruits gently, late summer, early autumn. Bring in before first frosts and ripen inside if necessary.	Slugs, potato blight if grown near potatoes.	Cordons climb and need support. Bushes are free-standing but need a mulch of straw to stop fruit lying on soil.

Fruit

Fruit divides into two main groups – top fruit, which is mostly grown on trees (like apples and pears) and soft fruit, which is grown on canes and bushes (usually some kind of berry). Soft fruit is covered in detail below. Strawberries are low-growing, short-lived perennial plants and fall into the category of soft fruit although they have slightly different requirements.

As fruits are longer-lasting plants than vegetables, it is very important that you pick a suitable site. It must be sunny and the soil should be well nourished and free of weeds. You should feed the plants well every spring with specialist tree and shrub fertilizer and ensure that you provide plenty of water both when the plant is growing and when the fruit is swelling. It is also important to prune the plant correctly, particularly during its early years. There are surprising differences in the treatment of the various types of fruit and these are listed below. Looked after well, most bush and cane plants should produce fruit for seven years and trees for much longer.

Problems

The factors that can adversely affect fruit crops seem endless at first glance, but in fact many are easily avoidable.

Site
If your plants are poorly situated they will not thrive. They need a sunny, sheltered spot with a well-nourished, well-drained soil. Fruits are much less tolerant of deficiencies than most other garden plants.

Water supply
If their roots are allowed to dry out at any time, the plants will suffer. Unlike many other shrubs, fruits need a regular supply of water rather than a soaking every one or two weeks.

Weather conditions
You will have little control over it, but the weather can seriously affect your fruit crop. Trees are at particular risk from frost, especially early-blossoming fruit trees like pears. It is obviously impossible to cover an entire pear tree, but strawberries and smaller bushes and canes should be covered with newspaper or polythene if at risk. Remember the better the blossom, the better your fruit will be.

Thinning the crop
The fruit itself can cause problems if the crop is too heavy. Branches may be damaged or even broken and the individual fruits may be small. Do not be tempted to think that a lot of small fruits will be any good. Usually

the smaller the fruit the less developed it is and the less flavour it will have.

Pruning
Bad pruning can also affect the crop, especially on canes. It can usually be remedied by subsequent prunings, but you may lose a year's fruit. Individual instructions are given under the various fruits.

Harvesting
Harvesting must be done with care since it is easy to damage the plant at this stage. Techniques vary from crop to crop, but as a general rule if you are cutting stalks you should make a neat cut with secateurs rather than pulling at the fruit. Equally, if you are picking the fruit itself, always twist it gently to make sure it is ripe and ready to be harvested. If you pull it away roughly you may damage the remaining spurs and stems and prevent the other fruit in the cluster from ripening. Ideally you should harvest every two or three days so you collect each piece of fruit at the optimum moment.

Pests and disease
Fruit can be prey to various pests and diseases but most of these should not be too serious a problem if they are dealt with early on. Birds are a very persistent threat and it is probably easiest if you just accept that you will have to share part of your crop with them. A net is the best deterrent and should enable you to save most of the crop (see the section on soft fruit below). Slugs can destroy an entire strawberry patch, but a mulch will usually keep them off. Diseases are covered under the various fruits.

Plant development
The final factor that may affect your crop is the age of the plant. Most fruit trees do not produce fruit for the first three years and then the initial crop is usually small. For bushes and canes, the first crop after planting is usually poor while the plant concentrates on settling in. Old age is another factor that will affect the crop, with bushes and canes declining when they are between seven and ten years of age, and strawberries after three.

Soft fruit
Soft fruit divides into three groups – bushes, canes and strawberries. Bushes and canes are both permanent plants that need careful pruning each year, whereas strawberries are low-growing plants that die down each winter. Feeding, watering, training and pest and disease

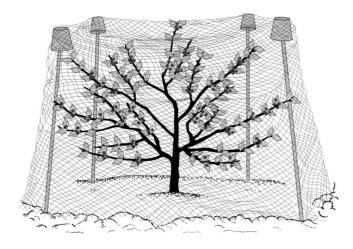

a net such as this is essential to protect all soft fruit

control are a continuous job for all soft fruit. Your plants will not die if you neglect them for a week, but constant care during the growing season will give you a much better crop. Netting for all soft fruit is essential unless you want to lose a large proportion of your fruit to the birds. For cane fruits you can attach a net to the trellis support and for other fruits you can easily construct a fruit cage. You can buy aluminium cages in various sizes or you can make your own. For a solid structure, put wooden posts in the ground round the edge of the area and nail chicken wire to them. Remember to leave a flap so you can get in and out! For a less permanent structure simply put tall canes (2 m/6 ft) into the ground around the bed, balance a flower pot on the top of each cane and drape the netting over them. You can then weigh this down with rocks or bricks.

Bushes
The main fruits in this group are gooseberries, blackcurrants, redcurrants and whitecurrants. Gooseberries, redcurrants and whitecurrants all grow up on a single stem and then spread out to form a bush at about 10 cm (4 in), whereas blackcurrants grow up on a group of stems.

Gooseberries
Both green and red gooseberries can be grown and are totally different from the fruits usually available in shops as you can wait to harvest them when they are perfectly

ripe. Most commercially grown gooseberries are picked when still unripe to make handling and storage easier.

Planting   Gooseberries like well-drained but not dry soil and do particularly well in moderate, damp climates with enough sun to ripen the fruit. They can be grown as bushes, cordons or standards. Standards or semi-standards are probably the easiest as the branches are clear of the ground, which makes weeding and harvesting easier and prevents suckers developing. Training gooseberries as a cordon requires quite a lot of work and diligent pruning. Late autumn is the best time to plant gooseberries but you can also do so in the spring. Prepare the soil well as you would for any shrub and plant bushes about 1.5 m (4–5 ft) apart. Cordons can be put 12 cm (1 ft) apart.

Care   Gooseberries like a feed of potash in winter or spring and a good 8-cm (3-in) layer of mulch in the spring. The mulch will reduce evaporation and help to retain water during the summer. Watch for any suckers and pull them up as soon as they appear, being careful not to damage the main roots. Pruning should be carried out in the winter and with bushes the aim is to create an open centre to the plant, which will make picking easier and reduce the chance of mildew by improving ventilation around the fruits.

Harvesting   For cooking, gooseberries can be picked in late spring or early summer. If you want to eat the fruit fresh as it is, leave it on the bush to ripen. Gooseberries can be frozen or made into preserves.

Problems   Gooseberries must be netted to protect the flowers and fruits from birds. Mildew can be a problem. Keep the bush well ventilated and cut away any branches the moment they begin to look powdery and you should keep the disease from spreading. Alternatively, plant the resistant strain 'Invicta'.

Diseases: rust, grey mould, honey fungus.

Red and white currants

Botanically red and white currants are part of the same plant *Ribes rubrum*. Both are easy to grow and will crop well as long as they are protected from birds.

Planting   Currants do best in full sun but will survive light shade. As with all fruits they like a well-drained soil that is not too dry. If possible avoid areas that are windy or prone to frosts. Plant in early winter preparing the ground as you would for a shrub. Make sure you plant level with the old soil mark on the stem. Bushes should be 1.5 m (5 ft) apart, cordons 45 cm (18 in).

Care   A good layer of mulch 8 cm (3 in) in the spring is beneficial as it will also reduce weeds. You should keep the area round the base of the plant free of weeds, but you must be careful when weeding as currants are shallow rooted. Red and white currants fruit on old wood and should be pruned in winter. For the first four years cut the new growth back by half in winter to establish a good framework. After that cut the side shoots back in summer and again, more fiercely, in winter to one bud. On the whole red and white currants are very unfussy and will produce fruit whatever you do to them; following the method above should simply give you more fruit.

Harvesting   Currants should always be picked as bunches rather than individual fruits. You can start to pick the fruits in early summer but they will not fully ripen until late summer or early autumn. They can be frozen or made into jelly.

Problems   Birds are the biggest problem but both they and mould can be prevented from damaging your crop (see above). Aphids and leaf blister can affect the plants but are not usually serious.

Blackcurrants

Blackcurrants are different from the other bushes as they are multi-stemmed. They also tend to be more sprawling and consequently take up more space in the garden unless you choose a compact variety.

Planting   Blackcurrants do best in full sun or light shade. They like rich soil so dig in compost before you plant. Ideally choose late-flowering varieties as they will be less susceptible to frost damage. The bushes are best planted in winter at least 1.5 m (5 ft) apart and should be put in the ground so the old soil mark on the stems is two inches below the soil level, as this will encourage growth. You should then cut the stems back to one bud above the ground. This will mean you do not get a crop the first year but will provide a better framework for the bush.

Care   Prune in autumn or winter and, as with other bushes, keep the centre of the bush open. Blackcurrants fruit on the previous year's growth so cut away any old or badly growing branches at the same time. You should aim to remove one-third of all fruiting stems each year so there are no branches more than four years old on the plant. Mulch in spring and, as with all soft fruits, provide protection from birds.

Harvesting Unless you are going to eat the fruits immediately, they must be dry when you pick them. The currants will be ready to pick in summer and will keep better than red and white currants as their skins are tougher. They can be frozen or made into preserves.

Problems As before, birds and mould can cause problems, also aphids and occasionally honey fungus. Weeds are less likely to grow round the base of blackcurrants because the bush spreads and creates an area of deep shade around its roots.

Canes

This group includes raspberries, blackberries and other fruits such as loganberries and tayberries. As their name implies, all these fruits grow on canes, which need to be supported on a trellis framework. You can either attach

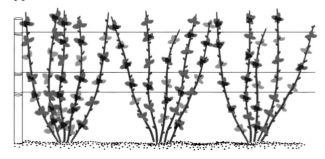

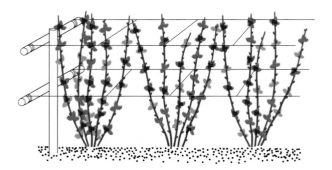

trellis for cane fruit

the canes to a single row of trellis or, if you have room, grow them between two parallel rows. A single row of posts 3 m (10 ft) apart will provide the basis for your trellis. Stretch strong wire in between them at 75 cm (2½ ft), 1.1 m (3½ ft) and 1.5 m (5 ft). Extra twine woven between the wires will make training the fruit easier.

If you have enough space, position a similar trellis 75 cm (2½ ft) away alongside. You can then criss-cross wire or string between the horizontal wires.

Raspberries

There are two main types of raspberry – summer and autumn fruiting. The autumn variety is a very densely-growing plant, which takes up more room but it is useful as it provides fruit at an unusual time and is not so attractive to birds.

Planting Raspberries like a moist, light, acidic soil – a pH of 6.5–6.7 is ideal. They do not do well on chalk and prefer a sunny site although they will do perfectly well in light shade. The one thing to avoid is too much wind. Raspberries should be planted in late autumn 60 cm (24 in) apart. After planting, cut the stems back to 23 cm (9 in) above ground as this will encourage new growth.

Care The plants should be mulched in early spring with a non-limey mulch (i.e. not mushroom compost as it is alkaline). Water the plants well in summer and pull up any suckers as soon as they appear, being careful not to damage the plants, which are shallow rooted. The canes should be pruned in summer after fruiting. Cut all the old canes to the ground and thin the new ones leaving six or eight. These will provide the canes for the following year's crop as raspberries fruit on the previous year's growth. After the winter trim the top of each cane by a couple of buds. An easy way to carry out the pruning is to grow the canes in a fan with the old growth at the sides and the new shoots trained straight up the centre. When you have cut away the fruited stems the new growth can then be spread out. Alternatively you can train the plant in a fan shape and cut out the alternate stems each year. If you choose this method you must train the new shoots carefully in between the old stems.

Autumn-fruiting plants should have all their old canes cut to the ground in winter and the new shoots thinned as they grow up. These plants fruit on the current season's growth.

Harvesting Summer fruits should be ready mid- to late summer and autumn fruits early to mid-autumn. The fruits should be dry when picked and should come away easily. Raspberries do not keep well and should be eaten or processed within hours of picking. They freeze well and make delicious jam.

Problems Virus-resistant varieties are now widely available so, if possible, choose one of these. Birds and squirrels are the main threats, but they should not pose a problem if you net the fruit. Cane spot and raspberry beetle maggots are the only other risks.

Blackberries

Blackberries are easy to grow but the plants can get large and will overtake your garden if left unchecked. On the plus side you get a large harvest of delicious fruit.

Planting Blackberries like a moist soil with no lime. They will do well in sun or partial shade and as they flower late, frost is rarely a problem. They can be planted any time from late autumn to early spring and should be placed 3.5 m (12 ft) apart. Blackberries can be trained along canes or grown through a hedge. After planting cut down to about 23 cm (9 in) to encourage growth.

Care Like most soft fruits, blackberries should be mulched in spring and given a good supply of water during the growing season. Blackberries fruit on the previous year's growth so cut out fruited canes after harvesting. At the end of the winter remove any frost-damaged tips on the new shoots.

Harvesting The fruits should be ripe in early autumn and should come away from the stem easily. The earliest fruits are usually the best and it is commonly thought that blackberries picked after the first frost will be sour as the Devil has spat on them! They can be eaten fresh, frozen or preserved.

Problems Blackberries have remarkably few problems. They produce so many fruits that there are usually enough to share with the birds, although if you want the entire crop you should net your canes. Virus-free plants are easily available and the only real problem – grey mould – is not that common.

Strawberries

Unlike other soft fruits strawberries have no woody growth. By planting a mixture of summer and perpetual strawberries you can have fruits from late spring to late autumn.

Planting Strawberries do best in a sheltered spot, either sunny or lightly shaded. They like rich, heavy soil and do not do well on chalk. For well-flavoured fruit add plenty of compost when preparing the bed. Also make sure you clear the area of weeds as young strawberries cannot compete against them. If planting as part of a rotation system in the kitchen garden, bear in mind that strawberries will not do well in soil that has had potatoes, chrysanthemums, tomatoes or other strawberries growing in it in the previous three years. Summer fruiting types should be planted in the late summer or early autumn and perpetual plants in autumn or spring. Plants grown in containers, such as strawberry pots, can be planted at any time as long as the weather is mild. You should leave 45 cm (18 in) between plants in the ground and ensure that the crown of the plant is just

fresh strawberries are just one of the rewards to be had from the kitchen garden

above ground level. To grow strawberries successfully you really need two beds that you can use in rotation. The plants usually live for three years so you can have one bed resting while the other is in use. This rotation prevents both soil exhaustion and the establishment of disease.

Care Strawberries benefit from a feed of potash and need watering well during the growing season, although you should avoid getting water on the fruits as they ripen since this will make them more likely to rot. The fruits should be protected by netting, otherwise you will lose your crop to the birds. Slugs and rotting can also be problems, but these can be prevented by mulching around the plants to keep the fruits off the soil. A thick layer of straw or strawberry mats will protect the fruits while they ripen. After harvesting remove the old foliage and cut the stems down to about 8 cm (3 in) above the crown. At the same time clear away the straw or protective layer.

During growth, runners will form off the main plant. You can either cut them away or peg them down into the ground to form new plants. By late summer they should have established their own roots and you can cut the plant from its parent. Leave the new plant for a week to recover and then you can replant it for use next year.

Harvesting Ideally you should harvest the fruit every few days as strawberries do not keep well once ripe and are prone to mould. Strawberries are best eaten fresh, but can be preserved as jam.

Problems The main pests are birds and slugs, which can be dealt with if you net and mulch the fruit. Frost can be a problem, but strawberry plants are easy to cover with newspaper if you think they are at risk. Grey mould might attack plants, but can usually be prevented from taking a hold if you remove any mouldy or fluffy-looking fruit and ensure the mulch does not become soggy.

Herbs

Herbs have been cultivated in gardens since ancient times for medicines, flavourings, cosmetics and perfumes. Although many are now grown for their flowers alone, like irises, traditionally the flowers were regarded as a bonus rather than the main reason for cultivation.

Herbs are not an isolated plant category, but come from all the different groups and can be found amongst bulbs, annuals, biennials, perennials, shrubs and even trees. A common definition of a herb is a plant that has culinary or curative uses, but this is a very loose description as many plants that can be classified as herbs are more usually regarded as flowers (like *Viola*) and vice versa.

Most herbs are extremely easy to grow as long as you provide the two conditions necessary for most of them – well-drained soil and a sunny spot. Most culinary herbs originate from the area around the Mediterranean and while they do not usually mind how poor the soil is, they will not grow well in damp or shady places.

Walled or enclosed gardens with geometrically patterned beds are what spring to mind for most people when thinking of a herb garden, but you could grow your own in a collection of pots by the kitchen door. Herbs will happily grow in a flowerbed amongst other flowers and can also be grown in window boxes. The size of your garden will obviously influence the scale of your herb growing, but if possible it is always worth having the herbs you need regularly for cooking within easy access. Even if you have a large herb garden, a few pots near the kitchen door as well can make life much easier. 'Fresh' herbs can be bought in supermarkets, but nothing can compare with cutting a few leaves from a plant and adding them straight to the cooking pot.

When deciding where to grow your herbs, sunshine is the single most important factor. You can always improve the drainage by digging grit, sand or organic material into the soil. Many herbs not only grow better in the sun, but also taste better as the sunshine brings the oils to the surface of the leaves giving them a more intense flavour. Look at the following chart to see the requirements of the herbs you wish to grow and plant your garden accordingly. Most herbs prefer to be sheltered from strong winds and this is why herb gardens are frequently enclosed within walls or thick hedges. Box can be useful for edging the beds as it provides shelter for the herbs and looks attractive. A small, sheltered herb garden with a sea of thyme and chamomile growing up between he paving stones can be delightful but you may not have the space for this. Many herbs are attractive to look at and can easily justify their position in a flowerbed. Others, such as sage, have small flowers but attractive foliage.

Herbs can also be successfully planted around roses; sage and lavender will complement the aromas whereas chives, a member of the onion family, will not only encourage the scent but also discourage greenfly. Aromatic herbs, such as chamomile, mint, lavender, thyme and rosemary are worth planting by a doorway or path where you will brush against them and release their scent. Chamomile and thyme can be planted in gaps in between paving stones where they will smell glorious as you step on them. Both plants will survive being walked on, but put them at the edge of a path rather than the centre so they are not subjected to too much rough treatment.

For many gardeners, the easiest way to grow herbs is in containers. This way you can get the soil mixture exactly right and can move the plants around easily. Many herbs need protection during the winter (see chart) and some can even be brought inside during the colder months. Put plenty of stones in the bottom of the container to ensure good drainage and then plant the herbs in ordinary potting compost. If you wish you can dig in extra grit and organic material, but this should not really be necessary. Herbs grow well together and three or four can be grown together in a pot or window box. Keep the plants well trimmed to encourage bushy growth and stop them becoming leggy. Feed them about once a month with a liquid feed during their growing season. From studying the chart you will see that many herbs can easily be grown from seed and although a lot die during the winter, some, such as parsley, mint, French tarragon and chives, will survive if potted up and put on a sunny windowsill.

Herbs: planting and care

Herb	Type	Where to plant	Propagation	General
Basil (*Ocimum basilicum*)	Tender annual	Sun, poor soil. Must be protected against cold. Often best on windowsill indoors.	Seeds, half-hardy annual. Plant in pots or plug trays. Do not over-water or expose to cold.	Water early in day, not evening, to avoid damp roots overnight. Pinch out tops of stems to encourage growth. Purple basil (*O.B.* var *purpurascens*) is attractive but not so good for cooking.
Bay (*Lauris noblis*)	Tree	Full sun. Protect from frost (below –5 °C/23 °F) and wind. Rich soil.	Cuttings taken in late summer. Can be difficult. Seeds slow. Easiest to buy small plants.	Will grow to 7 m (23 ft). Can be clipped into shapes. Put a layer of mulch around the plant in spring and do not let the soil dry out. Good in pots as they can be brough inside.
Bergamot (*Monarda*)	Perennial	OK in shade. Ideally semi-shade and rich moist soil.	Softwood cuttings or division in early spring. Remove centre after two to three years.	*M. didyma* has striking red flowers. Dies back in winter. Cut to ground in autumn and protect with mulch.
Borage (*Borago officinalis*)	Hardy annual	Full sun and well-drained, good soil.	Direct sowing after last frost.	Grows quickly and will self-seed. *B.O. alba* has white flowers rather than the ordinary blue or purple.
Chamomile (*Chamaemelum nobile*)	Perennial	Sheltered with sun and well-drained soil.	Divide in spring or autumn.	Water well during summer. Cut back in autumn.
Chervil (*Anthriscus cerefolium*)	Hardy annual	Semi-shade and moist soil.	Sow seeds direct in spring and summer.	Late sowing will produce leaves through winter in mild areas.
Chives (*Allium schoenoprasum*)	Hardy perennial bulb	Rich soil, best in sun but will survive in light shade.	Sow seeds direct in late spring. Divide in spring every three to five years.	The flowers are edible but the plant will do best if kept trimmed. Dies back in winter but can be potted up and kept indoors.

continued

Herbs: planting and care – *continued*

Herb	Type	Where to plant	Propagation	General
Coriander (*Coriandrum sativum*)	Hardy annual	Full sun, well-drained soil.	Sow seeds direct in spring through to autumn.	Leaves and seedheads can both be used. Will survive during winter in mild areas.
Dill (*Anethum graveolens*)	Hardy annual	Full sun, poor soil.	Sow seeds direct from spring to mid-summer.	Self-seeds. Do not grow near fennel as they will cross-pollinate. Water well.
Fennel (*Feoniculum vulgare*)	Perennial	Full sun, well-drained soil.	Sow seeds direct or divide in spring.	Self-seeds. *F.V. purpureum* has bronze leaves. Very attractive plant.
Feverfew (*Tanacetum parthenium*)	Perennial	Full sun, well-drained soil.	Sow seeds in pots in early spring. Divide in autumn.	Attractive flowers. Self-seeds. Trim in summer after flowering.
Lavender (*Lavendula*)	Shrub	Full sun, well-drained soil.	Softwood or semi-hardwood cuttings.	Trim regularly to prevent it becoming leggy. Do not cut into old wood. Great variety.
Lovage (*Levisticum officinale*)	Perennial	Sun or semi-shade. Rich, well-drained soil.	Sow seeds direct in autumn or divide.	Self-seeds. Trim during summer to produce new leaves. In three to five years will grow 2 m (6 ft) tall and 75 cm (2½ ft) wide.
Marjoram (*Origanum marjorana*)	Half-hardy perennial – best grown as annual	Full sun and well-drained soil.	Sow seeds in trays in spring or divide in spring or after flowering.	Also called sweet marjoram. French or pot marjoram is *O. onites* (small shrub).
Mint (*Mentha*), Spearmint (*M. spicata*), Applemint (*M. suaveolens*), Peppermint (*M. piperata*)	Perennial	Sun or moist shade.	Divide at any time.	Grow in a container or sink a bottomless pot around the plant in the soil to prevent it spreading uncontrollably. Great variety. Pot up and bring indoors for winter leaves. Trim during summer.
Oregano (*Origanum vulgare*)	Perennial	Full sun and poor soil.	Sow seeds in pots in autumn or spring. Divide in spring.	Also called wild marjoram. Plant gold-leaved varieties in semi-shade to protect leaves from midday sun.
Parsley (*Petroselinum crispum*)	Hardy biennial	Sun or semi-shade. Moist soil.	Seeds direct in spring through summer. Germination can be slow.	*P.C. neopolitanum* (French parsley) has flat leaves and stronger flavour. Remove flower heads.
Rosemary (*Rosmarinus officinalis*)	Shrub	Full sun, well-drained soil. Sheltered position.	Semi-hardwood cuttings late spring or early autumn.	'Miss Jessop's Upright' is neat, compact plant. Up to 2 m (6 ft) tall. Trim after flowering. Protect with straw in cold winters.

continued

Herbs: planting and care – *continued*

Herb	Type	Where to plant	Propagation	General
Sage (*Salvia offcinalis*)	Shrub	Full sun, well-drained soil.	Softwood cuttings mid-late summer.	Will survive mild winters. Prune in spring. Many varieties: purple (*S.O. purpurascens*), gold (*S.O. icterina*).
Tarragon (*Artemesia dracunculus*)	Perennial	Full sun, well-drained soil.	Divide in spring or take cuttings late spring–summer. Those labelled French seeds are sometimes Russian tarragon.	Russian (*A. dracunculoides*) is hardier but very little flavour. Cut back in autumn and mulch base.
Thyme (*Thymus*)	Shrub	Full sun, well-drained soil. Drought loving.	Divide in spring or take softwood cuttings.	Trim during growing season. Great variety. *T. vulgaris* is most common – 30 cm (12 in) high. Broad-leaved or Creeping Thyme *T. pulegioides* – 8 cm (3 in) high.

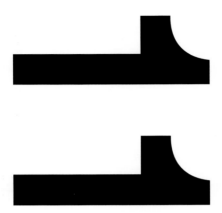

seasonal reminders

Mid-winter

- Mild weather is more dangerous than cold weather as plants can advance too fast.
- Look at the structure of the garden and plan any changes.
- Lawns: avoid walking on frozen or sodden grass.
- Containers: protect terracotta pots from frost. Ensure pots do not become sodden.
- Dig areas to be cultivated.
- Study seed catalogues and order seeds.
- Remove snow from evergreens.
- Plant deciduous trees and shrubs if mild.

Late winter

- Do not be misled by mild days. Water features, lawns, terracotta pots and tender plants are all still at risk from harsh frosts.
- Start sowing perennial and hardy annual seeds under protection.
- Pruning: prune roses and winter jasmine after flowering. Also ivy and shrubs that flower on new growth (see list on p. 66).
- Plant roses and deciduous trees and shrubs if mild.
- Put potatoes in boxes to chit. Sow broad beans, peas and spinach.

Early spring

- New growth appears and days lengthen but frosts and cold can still damage the garden.
- Weed and mulch after weeding.
- Sprinkle bonemeal around plants and dig in.
- Lawns: cut on highest setting when dry. Rake and aerate if necessary.
- A good guideline is that if the soil sticks to your boots, it is too wet to work or plant in.
- Bulbs: divide snowdrops. Deadhead bulbs but leave foliage. Plant summer-flowering bulbs.
- Divide and replant hardy perennials. Plant new perennials. Water all well.
- Pruning: prune roses, late-flowering shrubs (see list on p. 66) and spring-flowering shrubs after flowering.
- Plant deciduous and evergreen trees and shrubs.
- Plant chives and mint. Sow parsley.
- Plant potatoes. Sow carrots, lettuce, spinach, peas, beans.

Mid-spring

- Still a real danger of frost but you will need to water if it is dry.
- Continue to weed and mulch. Feed perennials, shrubs and roses.
- Pruning: prune summer-flowering shrubs. Prune spring-flowering shrubs when they finish flowering. Deadhead hydrangeas.
- Bulbs: deadhead, but do not cut foliage. Plant summer bulbs. Water all bulbs if necessary.

- Plant evergreen shrubs and all climbers.
- Lawns: feed lawn and cut slightly shorter.
- Plant sweet peas.
- Sow hardy annuals in situ.
- Plant perennials. Stake tall ones.
- Sow biennials.
- Plant potatoes and onions. Continue sowing vegetables for a staggered harvest.

Late spring

- Frost is still possible so be careful if planting out half-hardy plants. Tender ones are best left protected until early summer. Start planting containers indoors for summer displays.
- Plant hardy annuals.
- Mulch, weed, feed and water as required.
- Sow biennials.
- Bulbs: deadhead, but leave foliage. Plant tender summer-flowering bulbs.
- Stake all tall plants.
- Pruning: continue to prune spring-flowering shrubs. Prune *Clematis montana* and *C. armandii*, if necessary. Deadhead rhododendrons and azaleas. Clip box.
- Earth-up potatoes, stake peas, plant runner beans, continue to sow vegetables.

Early summer

- All danger of frost is now over. Water well as most rain will be lost through evaporation before it can sink into the soil.
- Weed and stake plants as necessary.
- Lawns: feed.
- Feed annuals with food such as tomato food to encourage flowers.
- Plant out tender annuals
- Pick sweet peas.
- Pruning: deadhead annuals, perennials and roses. Cut back early perennials to encourage new growth.
- Plant biennials for next year.
- Plant outdoor tomatoes. Continue sowing salad crops.

Mid-summer

- Most plants will need watering. Ensure the water reaches the roots and does not just evaporate off the leaves.

- Pruning: deadhead everything. Cut back perennials that have flowered. Trim deciduous hedges and then feed and water well.
- Stake where necessary and weed.
- Pick sweet peas.
- Tie in climbers, especially roses, as they put out new shoots.
- Bulbs: cut back foliage of daffodils and tulips. Lift and store tulips if you can be bothered!
- Sow last of biennials. Continue planting out.
- Trim herbs, earth up potatoes, sow salad crops, feed tomatoes.

Late summer

- Everything will still need watering. Secure plants against sudden fierce downpours.
- Weed, feed and deadhead.
- If going away, leave the lawn slightly longer in case it is very dry and move containers into the shade.
- Deadhead lilies and feed with tomato food for a good display next year.
- Bulbs: plant autumn bulbs.
- Pruning: prune wisteria and rambler roses. Trim evergreen hedges. Trim herbs and lavender after flowering but do not cut into old wood.

Early autumn

- May still need to water, but can also have early frost.
- Pruning: deadhead. Trim hedges.
- Clear annual bedding plants as they die off.
- Bulbs: plant spring bulbs.
- Plant biennials in situ.
- Plant evergreens.
- Lawns: mow grass, but do not cut too short. Feed and aerate if necessary.

Mid-autumn

- Clear up fallen leaves, especially on lawns.
- Bulbs: plant spring bulbs.
- Sow hardy annuals.
- Plant hardy perennials.
- Plant deciduous trees and shrubs. Check stakes and ties are secure on all trees, shrubs and climbers.
- Mulch using organic fertilizer.

- Protect tender plants and terracotta pots.
- Dig any areas of ground that have been cleared. The soil will become increasingly wet.
- Lawns: cut the lawn as necessary, leaving it slightly longer. It should be at least 2.5 cm (1 in) long for winter.
- Pruning: prune roses to prevent damage by wind.

Late autumn

- The garden will now be subjected to frost and possibly strong winds. All plants that are not fully hardy should be protected.
- Plant roses.
- Pruning: trim established roses to prevent damage by wind. Cut back perennials after flowering.
- Plant deciduous trees, shrubs, climbers and hedges. Stake and tie in well.
- Plant hardy perennials. Divide perennials if necessary. Protect half-hardy crowns with straw.
- Clear leaves.
- Lawns: do not cut lawns unless very mild and dry.

- Clear dead annuals.
- Dig soil.
- Bulbs: plant tulips.
- Finish planting wallflowers.
- Dig vegetable garden roughly. Winter frosts will break up the soil.
- Clean tools.
- Tidy the shed.
- Ensure fences and trellis are in good repair.
- Check water features for ice.
- Protect outdoor taps.

Early winter

- Clear snow off plants, especially evergreens.
- Dig new beds.
- Sweep leaves.
- Avoid walking on wet or frozen grass.
- Protect plants and terracotta plants from frost.
- Check water features.
- Read seed catalogues and plan for next year.

acid   Soil with a pH of less than 7.

aerate   Loosen the soil to allow more air into it, usually by spiking.

alkaline   Soil with a pH of more than 7.

alpine   A plant that naturally occurs above the tree line. Horticulturally it refers to plants that can be grown in rock gardens.

annual   A plant that completes its life cycle (germination, flowering, producing seeds and dying) within one year.

bare-rooted   Plants sold without soil around their roots.

bedding plants   Flowers that are planted out when almost mature to create a temporary display. Usually annuals, but can include biennials and perennials.

biennial   A plant whose life cycle is spread over two years. In the first year it produces leaf growth, in the second year it produces flowers and seeds and then dies.

bolting   Plants, particularly vegetables, that produce flowers and seeds prematurely, often due to drought or poor soil.

bulb   An underground stem that has modified to act as a storage organ. Usually consists of layers of scale leaves.

collar   The point where the roots meet the stem (also called **neck**) or on a tree where a main branch meets the trunk or a smaller branch meets a main one.

compost   Organic material created when vegetable and plant waste rot down. Also specialized growing mixtures available for particular situations, e.g. seeds, cuttings and containers.

cordon   Plant (usually fruit tree) pruned and trained to a single stem. Double or U cordons have two stems.

corm   Underground swollen stem or stem base. After flowering the old corm withers and a new one develops from it.

cotyledons   The first seedling leaf or leaves to appear once the seed has germinated. Often very different from mature leaves of the plant.

crown   The point on herbaceous plants where the stems meet the roots and new shoots are produced. Also the upper branched part of a tree.

cultivar   Variation of a plant produced by cultivation rather than occurring naturally in the wild. The characteristics will be retained when the plant is propagated.

cutting   A piece of stem, root or leaf that can be used for propagation.

deciduous   A tree or shrub that loses its leaves at the end of one growing season and re-grows them at the beginning of the next.

division   Splitting a plant into several smaller parts, each with roots and shoots, which will then re-grow.

dormancy   Period when growth slows down or stops, usually in winter.

drill   Narrow, straight, shallow furrow in the soil for planting seeds or seedlings.

ericaceous   Plants that will not tolerate lime in the soil and need a pH of 6.5 or less. Also used to describe compost in which these plants could grow.

espallier   Plant (often a fruit tree) trained flat against wires or a wall with a vertical stem and tiers of branches running off horizontally.

evergreen   A tree or shrub that retains its leaves throughout the year.

family   Plant classification of a group of related genera. Not usually given on horticultural labels.

fertilizer   Natural or synthetic plant food.

foliar feed   Fertilizer applied to the leaves.

fungicide   Chemical used for killing fungi, particularly those which cause plant diseases.

genus   Plant classification in between family and species. Based on the plant's botanical characteristics and indicated by its first Latin name. Plural: genera.

germination   Stage at which a seed becomes a plant.

grafting   Propagating by artificially joining one part of a plant to another.

ground cover   Plants that are usually low-growing and spread quickly to cover bare soil and suppress weeds.

half-hardy   Plants from warm climates that may need protection during winter in temperate areas. Usually tougher than tender plants.

hardy   Able to survive year-round outdoor conditions, including frost, without protection.

heel-in   Temporary planting until the plant can be put in its final position.

herbaceous   Plant that does not have a woody stem. Usually dies back in winter.

herbicide   Chemical used to kill weeds.

humus   Decayed organic matter that is vital for fertile soil.

hybrid   Offspring of plants of two different species.

inorganic   Chemical compound that does not contain carbon, i.e. not of plant or animal origin.

insecticide   Chemical compound to kill insects.

layering   Method of propagation whereby a shoot grows its own root system and can then be cut from the main plant to produce a separate plant. Self-layering occurs naturally.

loam   In many ways the ideal soil – easily worked, rich in humus and made up of equal parts of sand, silt and clay.

mulch   Layer of material placed on top of the soil to conserve moisture, suppress weeds and, in some cases, enrich the soil. May be organic (manure, bark, compost) or inorganic (black polythene or gravel).

neck   *See* collar.

nutrients   Minerals that are necessary in the soil for plant growth. The main ones are nitrogen, potassium and phosphorus.

organic   Substances with plant or animal origins, i.e. containing carbon. Also a method of gardening or farming that does not use synthetic or non-organic materials.

perennial   Plant that lives for more than three seasons.

pesticide   Chemical compound to kill pests.

pH   Refers to the acidity or alkalinity of the soil. pH7 is neutral, above is alkaline, below is acid.

pinching out   Removing the growing tip of a plant to encourage it to bush out.

plantlet   Small, young plant.

plug tray   Tray divided so that each seedling has its own compartment.

pollination   The transfer of pollen to stigma. Often carried by insects or the wind.

pricking out   Transferring seedlings from the container they germinated in to a larger one.

propagation   Making new plants from seeds, cutting, layering or division.

pruning   Cutting back plants to reduce size, control shape or increase flowering and fruiting.

rhizome   Fleshy stem that grows underground and acts as a storage organ, producing roots and shoots.

rootstock   Plant used to provide a root system for another plant that is grafted onto it. Often used for fruit trees so they will grow to a predetermined height.

seedbed   Level area of well-prepared soil set aside for sowing seeds.

seedling   Young plant that has grown from seed.

shrub   Woody-stemmed perennial plant. Usually branches out near the base with no single trunk.

species   Category of classification below genus, consisting of closely related plants. Abbreviation sp, plural spp.

spit   Depth of a spade's blade.

standard   Tree with 2 m (6 ft) or shrub with 1–1.2 m (3–4 ft) of clear stem below the first branches.

subsoil   Layers below the topsoil. Usually less fertile and of poorer texture.

subspecies   Subdivision of species, can be further divided into individual varieties. Abbreviation Subsp.

systemic   Pesticide or fungicide that spreads throughout the plant when applied to roots or foliage.

taproot   Main root that grows down into the soil from the stem. Can become large and fleshy and have other roots branching off it.

tender   Liable to be killed or damaged by cold weather or frost.

tines   The prongs of a fork or rake.

topiary   Creating shapes by clipping and training trees or shrubs.

topsoil   Top layer of soil, usually fertile. Depth can vary greatly.

tuber   Swollen underground root or stem used to store food.

variegated   Leaves marked with patches of another colour, most commonly cream, white or yellow.

variety   A smaller group of plants within a species, below subspecies. Abbreviation var.

Further reading

Plant encyclopaedias

Reader's Digest New Encyclopaedia of Plants and Flowers
Royal Horticultural Society A–Z Encyclopaedia of Garden Plants
Hessayon, Dr D. G. *The Expert Series*. The volumes on flowers, trees and shrubs and flowering shrubs are particularly useful.

Design

Colour

Hobhouse, P. *Colour in Your Garden*
Pope, N. and S. *Colour By Design*

Scent

Lacey, S. *Scent in Your Garden*
Verey, R. *The Scented Garden*

Perennial planting

Kingsbury, N. *The New Perennial Garden*
Ondolf, P. *Designing with Plants*

Water

Archer-Wills, A. *The Water Gardener*
Robinson, P. *RHS Water Gardening*

Plants

Pavord, A. *Plant Partners*

Cottage

Lloyd, C. *The Cottage Garden*

Wildlife

Baines, C. *How to Make a Wildlife Garden*
Verner, Y. *Creating a Flower Meadow*

Kitchen gardens

Biggs, M. *Complete Book of Vegetables*
Don, M. *Fork to Fork*
Flowerdew, B. *Complete Fruit Book*

Propagation

Thompson, P. *The Propagator's Handbook*
RHS, *Propagating Plants*

Organic

Flowerdew, B. *Complete Book of Companion Gardening*
Henry Doubleday Research Association *HDRA Encyclopaedia of Organic Gardening*

General authors

The following is a selection of gardening writers who have produced highly accessible gardening books. They are all individual in style and approach and the chances are that if you like one book by a particular author, then you will enjoy any other books he/she has written.

Beth Chatto, Monty Don, Charles Elliott, Marjorie Fish, Penelope Hobhouse, Gertrude Jekyll, Christopher Lloyd, Mirabel Osler, Eleanor Perenyi, Graham Stuart Thomas, Rosemary Verey.

Gardens to visit

The National Garden Scheme: This is a charity that organizes open days for gardens that are privately owned. These are listed in *The Yellow Book*, published each year in early spring by the National Garden Scheme. There is a separate scheme and book for Scotland.

The National Trust: Runs many important gardens. A yearly guide gives details and opening times. There is a Scottish National Trust.

The Good Gardens Guide: This is a yearly publication that gives details of the most important gardens open to the public, including selections from the above two organizations. It covers the whole of Britain.

These publications refer to British gardens, but most countries have equivalent organizations and guides. Tourist Offices or the Internet are good sources of information.

Plants

A huge range of books exists on individual plants from small pamphlets to multi-volume works. If you become interested in a particular plant it is worth visiting a specialist bookshop or library to find out what is available. You may also find gardens that specialize in that particular plant.

Internet

There are a huge number of gardening-related sites on the Internet, ranging from those devoted to individual plants or gardens to large commercial websites. Guides, such as *the good webguide: gardening*, are useful publications and it is worth remembering that many gardens and nurseries have their own sites. Below are one or two general sites:

www.crocus.co.uk

www.rhs.org.uk (Royal Horticultural Society)

www.hrda.org.uk (Henry Doubleday Research Association)

www.organicgardening.com

www.ahs.org (American Horticultural Society)

index